THE NEW ELITE

DAVID LEBEDOFF

THE DEATH
OF DEMOCRACY

THE NEW ELITE

A GROLIER COMPANY

FRANKLIN WATTS/*New York*/*London*/*Toronto*/*Sydney*/**1981**

A portion of this book appeared in
Esquire, August 1978, under the title
"The Dangerous Arrogance of the New Elite."

Library of Congress Cataloging in Publication Data

Lebedoff, David.
 The new elite.

1. Social classes—Political aspects—
United States.
2. Elite (Social Sciences)—
United States.
3. Democracy. 4. Political psychology.
5. Tradition (Philosophy) I. Title.
JK1788.L4   306'.2'0973   81-7473
ISBN 0-531-09854-0   AACR2

TO MY WIFE, RANDY

CONTENTS

THE NEW ELITE

FOREWORD

About fifteen years ago I became active in politics, which in my home state of Minnesota, was still a respectable thing to do. Through this activity I met people in every part of the state, from the most varied backgrounds. I found that each distinct community is really part of a whole. I saw the connections between people and the similarities. And I was able to appreciate a political system, however imperfect, that attracted able young persons to public life and provided citizens with a perceivable link to their own destinies and to each other. It was not heaven, but it worked.

It works no longer. Now nothing seems to work very well. As I saw things start to go wrong, and then get worse, I tried to identify the problem. People seemed to be losing their faith in all our institutions, and their sense of kinship with one another. The feeling of community was vanishing, and the sense of possibility, too. Why was this happening?

This book suggests a reason. So many of the things that have gone wrong in recent years may be related to a single cause: the growth of a new class and its pervasive alteration of society.

I think that what I call the New Elite is indeed the problem. Its impact has been tragic. But, *pace* Aristotle, there can be tragedy without villains. People can do bad things without being bad themselves. If good people—well-educated and intelligent—do foolish and destructive things, the fault must lie not with their heads or hearts, but with their vision. It behooves us all to try to make that vision less narrow.

CHAPTER 1
THE NEW ELITE

It was time for Thomas to get married. He was almost eighteen, his father had died, and the patch of land was now his. He needed a wife to help with the work, to cook and sew and bear children. He needed a wife as much as he needed the sun and the rain and the protection of his feudal lord. He wanted companionship, too, and sex. His needs were urgent and could not be postponed.

The problem was finding a bride. In Thomas's limited world there were three single women of marriageable age. One was sickly, one was strong, and one was beautiful. He married the one who was strong. There was really no other choice. The sickly woman could not work his poor land, and the beautiful one did not want to. She had other alternatives.

Thomas's bride was named Katherine. The couple got on very well, which is to say that even when not stupefied by labor they seldom fought with one another. He never regretted choosing her, nor she being chosen by him. They seemed to be compatible.

Neither Thomas nor Katherine ever wondered who was smarter. Intelligence was not a factor in marital selection. There was no such thing as an IQ test. No one even suspected that intelligence could be measured. There would have been no point to such measurement. Intelligence was not related to one's station in life. There was no social or economic mobility. A person was born to a certain role and stayed there. The great majority of people spent their lives on the land in harsh drudgery.

As it happened, Katherine was much the brighter of the two. Using the numerical scale with which we are familiar today, Thomas had an IQ of 105 and Katherine's was 147. This means that Thomas's intelligence was very near average (100) and Katherine's in the "genius" category. Neither suspected this disparity. Both were illiterate. Almost everyone was. The conditions of their lives did not recognize, let alone reward, Katherine's special gifts.

Thomas and Katherine lived in England in the twelfth century, but the circumstances of their union would have been much the same in Italy or Russia or China, in the Middle Ages or the Renaissance. From the dawn of time until the eighteenth century, the process of marital selection was very much the same. Spouses were chosen from the very small pool of those who happened to live nearby. They were chosen without regard to, and without any way of knowing, what their general intelligence might be.

Until fairly recently, intelligence was randomly scattered throughout the population. Almost all people were peasants, and that included most people with high IQs. Some members of the tiny ruling class were undoubtedly brighter than the average, just as some others most assuredly were not, but that class was so small that its composition could not affect the general distribution of intelligence throughout the total population. By and large, intelligence had nothing to do with one's station in life. A genius comparable to Einstein could die illiterate after a lifetime of serfdom in the fields. No one knew of his ability, and no one would have cared.

Two biological truths remained constant throughout human history until the modern age: (1) intelligence was randomly distributed, and (2) people mated without much regard to the intelligence of their marriage partners. The second truth assured the continuity of the first. A man and woman, each with an IQ of 150, will very probably produce children who are brighter than average, but (also probably) not quite as bright as their parents. The tendency is for the offspring to move back toward (or up toward) the average. This is known as regression toward the mean. If one of the children had an IQ of 140 and married someone with an IQ of 160, *their* child might have an IQ of 150. That is to say, if bright people continue to marry only bright people, their children will continue to be bright, and the principle of regression toward the mean can be avoided.

But of course this did not happen. With regard to the matching of their IQs, people married just as arbitrarily as did Thomas and Katherine. Biologically, it was close to a purely random selection. It was extremely unlikely that any of Thomas's and Katherine's great-grandchildren would have IQs as high as Katherine's.

In the modern age all of this changed. The change began only a few hundred years ago, but it has already altered irrevocably the patterns of human life on this planet. For the first time in history, intelligence is neither randomly distributed nor transmitted.

Three factors account for the change. First, there is greater mobility now; the search for a spouse need not stop at the farm next door. After the Industrial Revolution, most people did not live on small, isolated farms but in cities and towns. Aldous Huxley observed (at the time, people thought he was jesting) that the most important invention in history was the bicycle because it meant that a person could reach, and therefore choose, a spouse from several dozen possibilities rather than two or three.

This is not to say that people could marry whomever they wished. The young suitor of the eighteenth, nineteenth, and early twentieth centuries was still likely to confine his search to women of his own social and economic background. He may have been more interested in a woman's physical appearance and/or her dowry rather than her mind, but the expansion of choice permitted him to choose someone whose company he enjoyed. This was an important new factor in selection. If the couple shared the same interests and enjoyed each other's conversation, the chances were improved that their intelligence might be roughly the same.

Second, universal education has become the rule in the Western world. If everyone can read and write, everyone can be graded and tested. Children can be told precisely how smart they are supposed to be, and that information, coupled with the resultant self-image, helps determine the choice of a spouse.

Third—and by far the most important—is that today, intellectual ability is rewarded. This is something very new in human history. Until very recently, real equality of opportunity did not exist. Now, by and large, one's ability *is* relevant to one's station in life, and people *can* rise to the level that their talent permits. The son of a cobbler is not necessarily destined to be a cobbler himself. He might be an accountant. And he might marry the daughter of a shopkeeper. People still tend to marry within their social and economic class, but membership in that class has come to depend more on measurable intelligence and less on circumstances of birth. A natural selection by ability has taken place.

The pace of this progress at first was very slow. Even in the United States in the early part of the twentieth century, intelligence generally remained randomly scattered throughout the population. Most people were members of what was called the working class; for them, equality of opportunity remained out of reach. It was still true that there were poor neighborhoods inhabited by many individuals of high general intelligence— whether they knew it or not—who spent their lives working in menial and low-paying jobs.

In the last three decades, however, the situation changed dramatically. Equality of opportunity for white Americans became the norm, not the exception. A white American of high intelligence might not become rich, but was likely to achieve at least a comfortable income. He or she would almost certainly receive a college education, and would enter a social and economic class composed of others with similar ability. There were—and continue to be—exceptions, but the general rule became well-established and its results observable.

It was not simply a small elite that was removed from manual labor. Millions of Americans performed skilled work for which they were well paid. Their positions were won by ability. Most individuals of high IQ had traveled to a station where they worked and lived with other individuals of high IQ. They married within this station, as did their children. For the first time in history, there was no regression toward the mean. Equality of opportunity meant that people were socially and economically stratified by virtue of their intelligence.

Some commentators feel the change is even more profound. Professor Richard Herrnstein of Harvard has written that "The message is so clear that it can be made in the form of a syllogism:

1. If differences in mental abilities are inherited, and
2. If success requires those abilities, and
3. If earnings and prestige depend on success,
4. Then social standing (which reflects earnings and prestige) will be based to some extent on inherited differences among people."

Herrnstein's syllogism has drawn some angry criticism because it assumes that intelligence is largely heritable, and this assumption has not yet been demonstrated to the satisfaction of all.

But the syllogism need not depend on the assumption that intelligence is largely hereditary. Environment may play a very important role. The syllogism stands, however, because children of intelligent parents are usually raised by those parents. They grow up in an environment molded by those of high IQ. Whether heredity or environment makes the most difference is debatable; children whose parents have high IQs tend to have high IQs themselves. The correlations of this result are clearly established; nature and nurture are really beside the point of the syllogism. Perhaps it should be restated:

1. If differences in mental ability are transmitted genetically and environmentally, and
2. If success requires those abilities, and
3. If earnings and prestige depend on success,
4. Then social standing (which reflects earnings and prestige) will be based to some extent on differences among people which are transmitted genetically and environmentally.

If this stratification has indeed taken place, then the implications for our society are greater than those of any revolution that has ever occurred. What is happening now has never happened before, and its most ominous result could be the death of democracy.

The princes and generals who once ruled the West did not justify their sovereignty on the grounds of superior intelligence. Indeed, for them "intelligence" had quite a different meaning. An individual might be called "clever," but that was not necessarily a compliment; it connoted a form of shrewdness close to trickery. Some rulers were known as "wise"—a more favorable appellation—but the reference here was to judgment, not intellect. What was meant was a sort of articulated common sense.

Whatever word was used, it had nothing to do with the right to govern. That was determined by force. It was not necessary to state that "might made right"; it was an obvious truth. The winners of the battle ruled the rest. What was carved out by the sword was retained thereafter through the force of habit and custom: Sovereignty was hereditary until some new power took it away. Of course, monarchs and peers whose station was derived from birth felt the need to justify the order that assured their succession, and they did not claim that that justification was the capacity of their brains. Instead, they endorsed less vulnerable theories, chief among them the divine right of kings. It was the Lord's will that they should rule. The sovereign was carrying out his role in the ordained scheme of things. The aristocrats were able to justify their position, too. They saw the key as training, not capacity. They had been trained from birth in the arts of governance, which their hereditary privileges permitted them to exercise with relative disinterest. When a new class arose, moneyed but untitled, it explained its share of power in terms of property; those with the greatest stake in society would be most vigilant in its preservation. None of these rationales had anything to do with individual characteristics.

Approximately two centuries ago, however, things began to change. A new idea called democracy struck the tinder of revolution and, in an amazingly short time, became the accepted goal of the peoples of the West.

Democracy rests on the belief that all persons are created equal. This view of equality does not mean that all persons have the same ability, but rather that ability is randomly distributed. This is regarded as so obvious as to be beyond dispute. Equality is presented as an observable truth, held to be self-evident.

And it was. Everyone knew that the cobbler was more intelligent than the prince, or rather, that some cobblers were more able than some princes. Even some princes realized that truth, but if they noticed that their tutors or their tailors had better minds than they, they did not see how that affected their role in society. That role was determined by God, custom, training, or the need for a stable order. There was no point to the fact that some people of low station had superior intelligence, just as there was no point to the fact that some people, of all ranks, were left-handed.

It is important to note what was new about democracy. It was not the observation that ability is randomly distributed. It was the attachment of political significance to that observation. The political significance attached to the fact that all people are created equal is, therefore, that all people should be permitted to govern. The will of the majority should prevail.

Majority rule was the radical message of democracy. At first, it was a limited message, the franchise restricted to propertied males. Only a minority of the real populace could vote, but within that minority the majority prevailed. The idea became fixed and was adhered to, while the definition of citizenry slowly expanded. Eventually it was a true majority that had the power to sanction social change.

The idea was not merely that the majority must decide. By itself, that idea would have been only a variant of the old concern for social order, this time buttressed by consent. At the heart of the doctrine of majority rule was the express conviction that the majority was right. The majority *should* rule, because it knew best.

But sometimes it seemed that the majority was wrong. Certain decisions were discredited by subsequent events. When this occurred, the true majoritarian did not abandon his basic faith. There were explanations for the error. The people had not been given all the necessary facts; crafty leaders had betrayed the people; the circumstance of crisis had precluded careful thought; the question had not been put properly. Despite or perhaps because of these excuses, the idea of majority rule was generally held to be consistent with the retention of broad powers by elected representatives. Those representatives had only to face the approval of the voters on a regular basis. When things went wrong, it was assumed that the representatives had been out of touch with the will of the majority. The correction lay in their replacement.

Almost everyone used to believe this. It was the most basic assumption in political life. And it was not only the majority that believed in majority rule; the minority usually held with it, too—even that tiniest of minorities, the intellectual elite. Liberal intellectuals not only gave lip service to majoritarianism; their commitment to it was heartfelt, outspoken, and profound.

To some this was surprising. On the surface, it might have seemed strange that highly educated people—college professors, for example—should place their faith in the judgments of the many. But liberal intellectuals in the Western democracies had always been most acutely aware that they had something very important in common with the mass of people: powerlessness. They saw that real power had always been vested in the rich; it was the inheritors and managers of corporate and private wealth who were solidly in control. The only effective force that could counter this power was the will of the majority.

In America, many liberal intellectuals had the best possible reason for assuming that members of the working class would be their allies: the intellectuals themselves had just emerged from that class and still shared many of its values. They did not talk about The People in an aloof and abstract sense; they *knew* the people, or felt they did. Those people were their childhood friends, their relatives. Belief in the wisdom of The People was almost an article of faith.

That faith also included the advancement of racial minorities and the protection of civil liberties, but there was no inconsistency in this. A written constitution that gave absolute protection to certain minority rights, regardless of the popular mood, was really a corollary to the belief in majority rule.

That belief, that faith, was nowhere as pronounced and fervent as in the United States. And this was true at least until the end of the Great Depression. It was the theme of all those Frank Capra films. The Common Man was his constant hero; his villains were the rich—owners of factories, of vast tracts of land, and very significantly, of newspapers. The quintessential Capra villain—the majoritarian Antichrist—was the newspaper publisher in *Meet John Doe*. The newspaper prevents the public from knowing the truth, the publisher disseminates slurs about John Doe, and the decent majority is thereby confused. When the hero tries to speak to the public directly—at a huge rally—the publisher's goons cut the microphone wires and no one can hear the speech. The newspaper as antimajoritarian force is portrayed just as vividly in Capra's *Mr. Smith Goes to Washington,* where a United States senator acts on the orders of a corrupt publisher and ignores the public will. These films were immensely popular in the 1930s; their description of a society in which the majority is the defender of virtue and justice against the manipulations of the rich and privileged was consistent with the attitude of most liberal intellectuals.

But after World War II, this began to change. A new law was passed that may have altered American society more than any other piece of federal legislation in our history. It was known popularly as the GI Bill of Rights. The generous response of a grateful postwar public, it provided tuition money to any returning veteran who was able to go to college. There were twelve million returning veterans, and an extraordinary number of them took advantage of the new law. Immediately, the percentage of Americans who attended college doubled, and shortly thereafter it doubled again. There were millions of new students on the campuses, most of them from economic backgrounds that once would have precluded college attendance. Academics braced for the assault. Deans and professors consoled one another over an anticipated decline in standards, but the results astonished them. The new students were very good indeed. As a class, they were as good as the upper-income students, whose tuition was paid by their families. It was undeniably clear that general intelligence— or at least the ability to obtain good college grades—was very widely distributed throughout the American population, on all economic and social levels.

More significantly, higher education was no longer the privilege of the chosen few. Millions of Americans now saw it as their right; before long, it was regarded almost as a prerequisite to a decent job and income. Campuses were expanded and new colleges built to accomodate the change in national expectations.

However, the principle established by this was not that all Americans have a right to a diploma but, rather, that every person has the right to be educated to the best of his or her ability. The poor might be just as qualified for higher education as the rich; it was just a question of finding *which* poor were qualified. It became a matter of testing. Once the proper tests were devised and given to all children, the ablest could be identified, and educated accordingly. Money was no longer an insurmountable barrier. Vast new scholarship programs had supplanted the GI Bill. Suddenly, the only barrier to (white) Americans who wanted to continue their schooling was their own ability. A previous generation had jokingly asked, "If he's so smart, why isn't he rich?" The postwar generation was more inclined to see it this way: "If he's so smart, why isn't he educated?" There were, of course, obvious examples of brilliant achievers—business executives, inventors, statesmen, even a president—who had not attended college. But they were older and they had been raised in a different era.

The testing programs worked very well. The brightest boys and girls, no matter what their background, swarmed to the campuses, there to win their diplomas and find their careers. It should be noted that "brighter" and "more intelligent" are used here for convenience only, as synonyms for "having higher IQs," even though it is understood that IQ tests probably measure only some aspects of intelligence, such as verbal skills, and certainly contain a cultural bias that unfairly penalizes those from deprived backgrounds. The point is not that the tests are accurate—they are not—but that they are mistakenly *believed* to be accurate and are therefore self-fulfilling. *Something* is being tested, and our society wrongly assumes that that something is general intelligence. The possession of that something, many people are told, makes them superior to others. That something is also rewarded by society. And that something *seems* to be heritable, though it may be transmitted in significant part through environmental factors.

So, young people with higher IQs were first identified and then segregated on campuses during the same years in which many of them choose their marriage partners. It was understandable that they would choose each other. For the first time in the history of this planet, stratification by IQ was almost assured. The boy with an IQ of 137 married the girl with an IQ of 141. Their children might not have IQs as high as those of either parent—because of the natural tendency toward the mean—but their intelligence would almost certainly be higher than the average. These children are members of the new class, too, educated as highly as their parents and likely to mate with others of similar background. The new class is therefore self-perpetuating, and it seems to be permanent.

This new class is self-segregated as well—particularly by association. Once its members are off the campuses, they usually work and live only with one another. When there is contact with others, the outsiders are usually in subservient roles—janitors, domestic help, gas station attendants, taxi drivers. The greater number of outsiders—those who punch time clocks in factories, for instance—are never seen at all. It is impossible to exaggerate how insular this new class is. Its members talk only to one another. They have little awareness of what the rest of the country is like.

The emergent class of those who believe themselves to be measurably brighter than everyone else can be known as the New Elite. A novelty in human experience, it is (except for the Chinese Mandarins) the first powerful social class in history whose membership is defined by measurable intelligence. Everyone not in this class can be referred to—in terms of the way the New Elite sees them—as the Left Behinds.

These terms are not near synonyms for older labels. The New Elite and the Left Behinds have no direct relationship to other pairs of confrontation: liberals and conservatives, Democrats and Republicans, upper-middle class and lower-middle class. Correlations may be made, but they are misleading and quick to change. One need not have attended college to be a member of the New Elite; a privileged dropout qualifies. A professor of philosophy at Princeton could easily be one of the Left Behinds if his or her basic identity is with a traditional social or economic or ethnic group. *The deciding point in every case is how individuals see themselves*. If an individual has strong roots in a social class or religion, in the values of an urban neighborhood or the farmland or country club life, then the fact that one's intelligence has once been measured as above the average may not be a critical point in self-identify or allegiance. But if such roots are absent, or if they have been rejected, one may assume a self-identify as an individual of measured superiority and find a class allegiance with other individuals of similar measurement. There is no admissions committee for either the New Elite or the Left Behinds. Each person is automatically a member of the class to which he assumes he belongs.

You can't be a member of the New Elite unless you see yourself primarily as intelligent rather than as something else. We all tend to think that society could benefit from the counsel of people like ourselves. Those who, when they say "ourselves" mean those with the highest measurable intelligence, are members of the New Elite. Those who when they say "ourselves" mean anything else—other businessmen or scientists or artists or women or Catholics or liberals or conservatives or Texans or Frenchmen or laborers or Mayflower descendants or farmers or dukes or millionaires or We the People—are members of the Left Behinds. Rejection of roots is a prerequisite for membership in the New Elite; adherence to roots (or class or caste or faith) is the primary barrier to such membership.

Sometimes one can tell the New Elite from the Left Behinds by what they do for a living. Care is required, however; occupation alone is not an infallible guide. And it's not simply a question of how much intelligence is required to perform a certain job. What really counts is whether the job is based on certain testable skills. Doctors, lawyers, architects, academicians,scientists, certain types of executives, many levels of government bureaucrats, some journalists, and others who deal in verbal skills, have all met the threshold test for the New Elite. But it must be remembered that it's only a *threshold* test; any members of those professions may be Left Behinds—if that's how they see themselves.

People whose work does not require professional, verbal, or technocratic skills are probably Left Behinds. This includes most small businessmen, retailers, manufacturers, manual and clerical workers, and salespeople. In a large corporation, the top executives and the assembly line workers are typically Left Behinds, and the upper-middle ranks—analysts, lawyers, researchers—belong to the New Elite.

The New Elite ranking of job status is based on how removed a person's work is from ratification by the public. Those whose success or failure is judged solely by their professional peers are likely to be part of the New Elite. Those whose success depends in part on public approval are Left Behinds. Salesmen are an obvious example, and so are most businessmen. Using the public ratification test, the most Left Behind occupation of all should be holding elective office—or at least this used to be the case.

The New Elite feels that it's good to have money, but not too much. It knows that really great wealth is seldom the salaried reward for testable technical and verbal skills. The nuclear physicist makes much less money than the owner of a uranium mine. Since great wealth suggests an occupation divorced from testable skills, the New Elite cultivates a life-style that connotes modest prosperity, not opulence. A Volvo wins more points than a Cadillac; a mink coat at a faculty party is a social disaster. The supporters of the recent John Anderson presidential campaign, many of whom seemed to be members of the New Elite, were often derided as the "wine and brie set." That taunt was not without significance; it helps locate its target on the economic scale: wine and brie are not beer and pretzels, but neither are they champagne and caviar.

The real significance of the New Elite is political. Its members are the managers of society—teachers, commentators, planners, officials, and executives—the articulators of thoughts and standards. In a society that rewards ability, the New Elite possesses influence far out of proportion to its numbers.

But it does not have political control. It has political power, certainly, but not political dominance. Democracy is based on majority rule, and the New Elite does not constitute a majority. To be sure, it is a large class and is growing while other classes are shrinking, but it's still a long, long way from 50 percent and knows that it's unlikely ever to enjoy majority strength.

At first this was not a problem. So long as many recent members of the New Elite shared some background and values with the Left Behinds, they shared the same political goals, too. Majorities were formed with members of both classes. But as time went on, the values changed within the New Elite. Now most of its members are not the children of the working class but the children of the New Elite.

Those who are economically comfortable see things differently from those who are not. They want different things. For example, they might be more concerned with halting inflation than with an increase in the laborer's minimum wage. Furthermore, the affluent can afford to be concerned about things other than economic survival, and to some extent can view the social issues of the day with relative disregard for their economic consequences. This permits them to be, or at least to feel that they are, freer in their thinking, more dispassionate and just.

The first great issue that split the two classes was the civil rights movement. The New Elite endorsed it, and the Left Behinds did not. More precisely, the New Elite was for much swifter and more comprehensive change. This was perfectly understandable, for nothing is more consistent with the New Elite experience than that individuals should be judged by their abilities as individuals rather than as members of a social class—or race. Many Left Behinds felt threatened by the move toward racial equality because they regarded their status and, in some cases, their jobs as protected by their color. Although not all New Elitists supported the civil rights movement, and although not all Left Behinds opposed it, the class dichotomy was clear. The result was that the civil rights movement made very considerable progress, but not nearly so much or so quickly as its advocates desired.

A second major issue was the war in Vietnam. Here, too, the new class lines were imperfectly drawn. Generally, the New Elite opposed the war earlier than the Left Behinds and was far more fervent in its opposition.

These two issues had a profound impact on the political perceptions of the New Elite. To some extent, its ideology had prevailed, but its efforts had also been frustrated, delayed and even, in particular skirmishes, defeated. The New Elite felt, correctly, that with regard to both issues it had been right, although it had faced what seemed at times to be not only opposition but opposition by the majority.

Both the civil rights movement and the peace movement had made efforts to win over the majority. Bright and principled young students had traveled to the South on behalf of racial justice and had rung doorbells in New Hampshire for the McCarthy presidential campaign. For the first time in many years, the New Elite was coming face to face with the Left Behinds. The meeting was not propitious. The Dartmouth junior rang doorbells, but he did not always like the people who came to open the door. They were usually not at all like the people to whom he was accustomed. They did not always share his point of view. And, as often happens when others don't agree with us, he thought that they were stupid. Everything in his experience supported this conclusion. Their grammer was faulty, their syntax laughable. If they read books and magazines, they were the wrong ones. Their taste was awful. They had pink plastic flamingos on their lawns and huge chrome gas eaters in their driveways. They were selfish, not altruistic; closed, not open; instinctive, not rational. They were stupid.

And, should anyone doubt that finding, there was always the obvious question: If they were so smart, how come they weren't educated? Before long, a corollary question formed in the minds of the New Elite: Why should one of *their* votes count the same as one of ours? It now was doubtful that the New Elite would endorse the values of a Frank Capra film. The newspaper publisher had become their class ally, and the common man something of a villian.

For the first time in the Western democratic tradition, many educated liberals no longer instinctively believe in majority rule. Subconsciously, they have begun to reject the most basic tenet of all. They no longer believe that all men are created equal. That was merely a way of saying that ability was randomly scattered throughout all levels of society, and they can see this is no longer true of measured intelligence. But so inbred in our culture is the conviction that the majority is right that the new disbelief has remained beneath the surface of awareness. It has permeated attitude but not yet conscious thought.

The members of the New Elite are engaged in doublethink. They give lip service to the majoritarian principle and even invoke it with passion on those occasions when their side outnumbers the opposition. While some believe that majoritarianism is right, in their actions they are antimajoritarian. In politics, their ceaseless strategy is inconsistent with their professed thought.

How can one profess to believe in majority rule and yet seek to subvert its results? The New Elite has developed a number of strategies for this purpose, and their use is growing. These strategies must be subtle enough to coexist with an expressed belief in what they seek to undermine and yet permit those who employ them to ignore this basic contradiction.

The easiest of these strategies is to identify a majority group and then claim to be speaking on behalf of all its members. A consumer advocate can claim to be speaking on behalf of all consumers, which is to say everybody. An environmentalist can oppose a new construction project in the name of all who live near the site. Never mind that a spokesperson has neglected to obtain the consent of those he or she "represents," and never mind that the majority in question exists only with regard to a specific characteristic or interest, its members sharing no consensus beyond that. But, of course, people *do* mind, which limits the effectiveness of this tactic and of spokespersons such as Betty Friedan and Phyllis Schlafly. This tactic is inconsistent with the majoritarian tradition in two basic regards. First, majority rule means *consenting* majority rule. Second, a true majority is an accumulation of individuals. Such groups have no political significance until their members express themselves as individuals. If the members of a group do agree with one another, then they will prevail—as a totality of individual expression. It is ironic that the New Elite, which sprung from the measurement and reward of individual ability, should seek to deny the role of the individual and instead find its focus in the arbitrary constructs of convenient groupings.

Another tactic is the growing reliance on the doctrine of negative consent. Here, a self-appointed spokesperson claims to be the democratically-elected representative of a special-interest group whose members are supposed to have given their consent. In fact, they have not. It works like this: The members of a group, such as all students on one campus, are informed that some individuals will be representing their interests. If a student does not want to be so represented, he or she must vote disapproval at a designated time and place. Unless this is done, it is assumed that the student has consented to the representation. This tactic is widely employed within the Public Interest Research Groups founded by the Nader organization on many campuses. Since many students either don't know about the negative option or neglect to exercise it, the resulting "representation" is extensive. Such negative consent lacks the element of true volition. It is similar to the marketing technique employed by some book clubs: Anyone who doesn't indicate by a certain date that the monthly selection is *not* desired will be billed for it. (These book club contracts have been attacked by Nader as unfair to consumers.)

Then there is the tactic of the Most Convenient Majority. (It can also be called the Doctrine of the Variable Whole.) This tactic *does* rely on the consent of a true majority, but a very small one. Suppose a new housing project is proposed for a large city and a majority of the few hundred residents near the project site oppose any new construction. The project is defeated. Perhaps several million citizens of the greater metropolitan area favored the project and would have benefited from it. No matter. Opponents can—and do—claim that a majority, however limited in number, sanctions their cause.

None of the methods described have been used directly in the political process. So far their employment has been limited to large interest groups other than political parties. The goal has been to achieve spokesperson status in representing those groups and to use that status to bring pressure on elected officials. When a local legislator is told that the lobbyist calling on him represents one million consumers or one hundred thousand students, he may believe those claims. It could make all the difference in determining his vote.

But real power goes far beyond lobbying. Real power is transferred in elections. From the New Elite point of view, this arrangement has a tragic flaw. In general elections, the candidate with the most votes wins. This might seem an insurmountable barrier, but an opportunity has been seen and has been grasped. Elections may be decided by the people, but the candidates are chosen by political parties. If the New Elite can gain control of one, or both, of the political parties, it can choose the candidate itself.

This is to be accomplished by changing the rules. The central tactic is to achieve political party rules that minimize majority participation, thereby permitting a small faction to gain control of the whole. This process is well under way; it helps explain the last few presential campaigns.

The rule changes that have produced the most outcry are the use of quotas and the misuse of affirmative-action programs. But the greatest restriction on majority representation has come from a different quarter: the use of various formulas to apportion delegate votes. Those formulas were meant to avoid the old practice of winner-take-all and to give each candidate a fair share of delegates. However, in the hands of the New Elite they serve another purpose. Now rules have been introduced that are so complicated and difficult that only graduate students can understand them.

The complexity of these rules poses the greatest threat to majoritarianism. There are several varieties of proportional voting, some of which are very complicated and not easily understood by the voters. They may not have been designed to be confusing, but that is their effect. The significant fact is that many of the rule changes are more confusing to some voters than to others; that is, they are much more of a problem for the Left Behinds than they are for the New Elite. Well-educated people may not be intimidated by lengthy voting instructions, but others may be so dismayed that they cease to participate in the process. The loss of these participants represents a critical and growing threat to our political system.

Majority rule means not just the number of votes that it takes to prevail but also the absence of restrictions on the right to vote. In internal party contests, the New Elite has sponsored rules and voting procedures so complex and time-consuming that they restrict the average person's role in party affairs. Senior citizens sit bewildered at precinct caucuses while the subtlest nuances of the Hare system are slowly intoned in redundant detail. A post office clerk leaves the meeting at midnight because the first ballot of the evening has not yet been taken and he must report to work by seven the next morning. Those who do stick it out may well decide never to return. Their right to participate has been effectively discouraged. Labyrinthine rules and lengthy meetings are the poll tax that the New Elite has been imposing on everyone else.

The damage to the caucus system at the hands of the New Elite is one reason for the sudden increase in the number of primary elections. Many states whose political parties operated under the caucus system have recently switched over to primaries, and the choice between caucuses and primaries has become a battleground between the New Elite and its opponents. This is particularly regrettable, because the caucus system—when properly conducted—was clearly compatible with majoritarian democracy. Arguably, it was better in this regard than was the primary.

Despite the assaults against it, rule by the majority is still safeguarded by most of our political institutions. Though partially eroded within the political parties, it remains the proclaimed and intrinsic norm of our society. Members of the New Elite continue to see their most cherished hopes and beliefs fail to proceed because they lack majority support. All their lives they have been accustomed to swift gratification of their wants and they are impatient now at the slowness of their efforts to gain political control. Reinforced by one another that their views are right, increasingly convinced that they will not become a numerical majority, they are beginning to openly attack not merely the procedures but the very idea of majority rule.

Their attack is, for the most part, indirect. Perhaps even now they do not recognize the implications. On a variety of fronts, however, they advocate positions that are incompatible with the assumption that the majority should prevail.

One of these positions has to do with moral right. The New Elite claims moral superiority in order to bypass the need for obtaining majority support. It holds that a view should prevail if the New Elite believes it to be morally superior to an opposing view, regardless of the number of people who support either side of the issue. A New Elitist thinks and says that "I and my friends should have our way on this matter because we are morally right. It does not matter that the majority opposes us because the majority is morally wrong. Moral right should prevail over numerical superiority."

This view does have some roots in our democratic tradition—roots, but not parallels. It was always understood that the decision of the majority might offend the consciences of some in the minority, and this possibility was respected. The majoritarian idea does not foreclose the role of private conscience. There is an honored place not only for moral dissent but for moral resistance, as there is a place for civil disobedience. But the idea has always been that moral resistance be used to convert the majority, not supplant it.

It is here that the New Elitists are breaking with tradition. Whether deliberately or through ignorance, they miss the point made by the advocates of civil disobedience. Thoreau did not seek to prevail but to resist. He understood that there were penalties attached to his dissent and that the payment of those penalties was an intrinsic part of dissent. It was in this fashion that one could honor personal conviction regardless of what the majority felt.

But the New Elitists read the classic texts more narrowly;

for them it is all Walden Pond and no Concord Jail. When their views are opposed by the majority, they seldom claim the right to carry out those views regardless of legal sanction. Nor do they often urge disobedience as a tool to change the majority's view. That would be to concede that the final decision is up to the majority. Instead, they claim that the majority doesn't matter, that the minority view should be accepted at once and by all because of its inherent moral superiority.

The use of moral argument has been reinforced by recent history. The New Elite *was* morally right with regard to racial equality and the war in Vietnam. In both areas it saw itself outnumbered, and in both it eventually won some success because the majority was persuaded of the merits of each cause. The moral argument was *accepted* by the majority. One might well conclude that the experience was an affirmation of democratic procedures.

But the New Elite saw it as an affirmation of moral protest. It applauded the tactic and not its response. The New Elite began to invoke a moral tactic in areas where its application is less apparent than issues such as war and race. The word *immoral* is now used by New Elitists as a simple synonym for *wrong*. Any view not in agreement with the New Elite is immoral. Graduate student delegates to a political convention in the Midwest denounce the use of pay toilets as immoral, and their peers applaud the description. It is no longer a question of converting the majority. The use of the word *immoral* is not intended to win arguments but to preclude them. It is a magic formula whose utterance is supposed to bring automatic support.

The word immoral is now debased through overuse; hence a priceless resource in the battle for liberal progress has been lost. It is not possible to mobilize the citizenry against political torture in Chile with the same vocabulary that is used to denounce those who don't buckle their seat belts.

Everywhere in America today, there's an assault on the idea that the people can determine their own policies. That assault has had

its effect on every institution in our society and on every branch
of government. It explains why so much decision-making has
been plucked from the legislative branch and dropped on the
federal courts. The rejection of the principle of judicial self-restraint coincided with the postwar rise of the influence of the
New Elite. The emergent class did not share Justice Felix Frankfurter's faith in the wisdom of the majority. Its members were
far more disposed to see weighty issues resolved by lifetime
judges, who were gifted people like themselves. So courts today
specify the number of showers and the amount of carpeting to
be used in public institutions.

There are still other tactics for the avoidance of majority
rule. There is the growth of support for "pluralism," the auton-
omous rule of specific constituencies. There is the effort to appropriate to one's cause all those votes that were never cast: "The
60 percent of the voters who stayed home were really supporting
me."

But the fact that the New Elite is grasping for power on
every front doesn't mean it has a specific platform it wishes to
impose. Aside from a vague desire to limit the growth of society,
to limit wealth and thereby weaken the link between wealth and
status, it has no program, no ideology, no agenda. The ultimate
political objective of the New Elite is not so much concerned
with *what* government does as with *who* does the governing. The
New Elite devoutly feels that what is best for society is that
society be governed by the New Elite.

In politics, what matters to the New Elite is not so much
what a candidate is for as who he or she is. The critical thing is
to find out whether the person is a New Elitist. Intelligence,
education, and views on the issues are not the only qualifications
necessary to win support. Again, these merely provide the threshold. What really matters is whether the candidate thinks that
human experience has a bearing on human problems. The New
Elite refuses to balance reason with experience. It enshrines the
former and rejects the latter.

In the New Elite's determination of whom to support, details
about the personal life of a candidate are very important. If he

worships regularly at the same neighborhood church that his parents and grandparents attended, he is likely to be in thrall to tradition—and vice versa. George McGovern impressed many supporters with his Japanese house. Life-style and appearance are thus very useful guides in determining who really belongs to the New Elite, and positions on the issues are almost irrelevant.

In politics, then, the New Elite is concerned with style over substance. The way to win over many of the best-educated voters is by emphasizing image, not issues. The Left Behinds, particularly the working class, are more likely to decide among candidates on the basis of the specific programs that they advocate, especially with regard to economic issues. But the Left Behinds, too, are increasingly concerned with image, desperately searching for candidates with the same roots, experience, and values that they themselves have known.

It is possible for a candidate to appeal simultaneously to both groups. John F. Kennedy is the classic case. Many Left Behinds supported him because they could identify with his roots—his religion, the closeness of his family, his pride in his immigrant forebears. They liked the fact that he listened to Kenny O'Donnell. The New Elite admired his style. They heard the accents of Harvard, not Boston. They liked his clothes and his wit, the quotes from Aeschylus, the cello concert in the East Room. They liked the fact that he listened to Arthur Schlesinger.

Thus, Kennedy could make the supposed missile gap with the Soviet Union the central thrust of his campaign without sacrificing the votes, or enthusiasm, of the New Elite—most of whose members were supporting reductions in defense spending. And he could become a champion of the civil rights movement without alienating a large working-class following, whose own views on race were often narrow. What the candidate says he's for now counts for much less than who he seems to be.

Sometimes even the same phrase, if carefully crafted, could please both audiences. The most popular line of Kennedy's inaugural address was "Ask not what your country can do for you, but what you can do for your country." Each side heard these words differently. For the Left Behinds, Kennedy was evoking the most traditional values: patriotism, discipline, sacrifice for the common welfare. For the New Elite, Kennedy was saying that the nation had no obligation to provide for the welfare of all its citizens; it had, in fact, a claim on their service for that which government itself determined was a proper cause of action.

What John Kennedy did is not possible today; a candidate can no longer placate both camps and attract a true majority. The impact of the New Elite on our political life has altered our politics beyond recognition. It dictated the choices, the style, the meaning, and the results of our last two presidential campaigns.

Everything that happens in American politics reflects the inroads of the New Elite or the reaction of the Left Behinds. Issues are almost irrelevant. Each new tremor in our public life is part of the battle between the two classes. Jerry Brown's enormous (initial) popularity is explainable by his simultaneous appeal to both classes. The blue-collar members of the Left Behinds see his abandonment of the governor's mansion as a repudiation of privilege; the privileged members of the New Elite view it as contempt for the material goals that are shared by most of the Left Behinds. The new class struggle explains as well the unexpected difficulties of the Equal Rights Amendment. A measure that is supported by a clear majority of Americans (and most respected persons in public life), it has been stopped by the nascent fears of the Left Behinds, who have learned to distrust every measure that removes from public control a matter of social concern. Examples are everywhere. The Dade County rejection of gay rights was probably directed less toward gays than toward those who scoff at traditional values—and insist that others do, too. Bella Abzug's defeat by a Republican in an overwhelmingly Democratic congressional district is yet another case of backlash by the Left Behinds against the New Elite.

And—oh yes—so is the victory of Proposition 13. That victory, and the national tax revolt that it has spawned, is much more than a protest against high taxes. Angry as people are at the tax rate, they're angrier still that it was levied without their consent. The real slogan of this new revolution is "No taxation without representation." The political process has been crippled in its capacity to serve as a responsive link to government; people sense that all the channels have been plugged. So when an opening occurs, even as wide and rough an aperture as the Proposition 13 ballot initiative, people rush to fill it with accumulated protest. Most of the voters of California knew that Proposition 13 was not a responsible answer to their problems. But they felt that the responsible avenues had been closed to them, and so they took the only opportunity at hand.

All the strange new activity of the last ten years represents the efforts of the New Elite to deny the democratic process. The vilification of political parties, the ascendancy of image over issues, the disrespect for law (which is a codification of majority will), the substitution of stridency for debate, of rallies for elections, or rigidity for compromise, the shifting of power from Congress to the courts, the growth of interest groups that bypass and disdain the political process, the self-appointment of spokespersons, the denigration of popular culture, the rejection of traditional values, the enthronement of the "expert," the enactment of rules that limit political participation in the name of extending it—all these things are rooted in the new belief that the majority does not, cannot, know what's best; that there exists a group that is measurably superior to everybody else; and that no statute or habit or procedure must be allowed to stand between that group and dominance.

Our society has scarcely become aware of the nature of the threat against it. That awareness should bring both the will and the strength to respond, because the New Elite is wrong in its perception of democracy. The majority *should* prevail. This is as true today as it was before the introduction of the Stanford-Binet Test. It will always be true. It is true because the capacity to make broad political choices is not related to measurable intelligence. This was assumed by those who wrote "all men are created equal." If that phrase had meant that measurable intelligence is randomly scattered throughout the population, then it would indeed no longer be true. But it did not. It meant that *ability* is widely scattered, specifically the ability to make political judgments. And that is as true now as always. The eternal truth is that political wisdom is not an attribute of intelligence or education or class or gender or race. It is the response to experience. In terms of the capacity to make political choices, the most significant response to human experience is the view one comes to hold of human nature. No one person or group has the right to define what human nature is. Each view is burdened by personal experience. We cannot prove, by logic or calculation, just whose version is correct. Only the majority knows, because only the majority view approaches the aggregate of human experience. We must mine the whole vein. We must ask everyone's opinion, and let the majority prevail.

CHAPTER 2

WHO ARE THE NEW ELITE?

Charlene's family was not exactly poor. They owned their own home—in Allentown, Pennsylvania—a modest but very well maintained house. There was always enough to eat and the children did not lack for clothing. Money was somehow found for birthday presents, holiday parties, and family outings at a nearby lake.

But there is not much joy in Charlene's recollection of her past, of which she remembers a great deal. She remembers having to wear her older sister's clothes, which, though clean and unpatched, were somewhat out of style. She remembers furniture that was nondescript, heavy, and cheap. She remembers that there were no magazines in her house, and very few books. She remembers being rather embarrassed, almost ashamed, when friends saw her neighboorhood, her home, her family. None of her grandparents were born in this country, and neither of her parents attended college. Charlene was distressed by the way her father spoke and annoyed by the narrowness of her mother's interests.

Charlene attended the public school nearest her home. It did not take long for her teachers to realize that she was a very gifted student. She received high grades and constant praise and eventually was encouraged to skip a grade; though younger than her new classmates, she continued to do superior work. The sciences and mathematics were her particular strengths.

By the tenth grade, Charlene discovered what she had had no opportunity to know at home: the beauty of classical music. She learned to play the violin. She also managed to build a large record collection, which she kept in her room.

Charlene graduated as the salutatorian of her high school class and received a science scholarship to Temple University in Philadelphia. Even with the scholarship, the costs of attending college away from home were high, so Charlene found a part-time job, and her parents volunteered to help out.

College opened up a whole new world to Charlene. Despite the fifteen hours a week she spent clerking at a drugstore, she was able to maintain outstanding grades. She found the time to make new friends and was delighted to discover others who shared her interests. Her new friends seemed far more stimulating than those she had left behind, and she felt proud to be accepted by them as an equal. There were so many things to do: concerts and lectures and long talks about them later. Charlene joined the Vivaldi club and also learned to play tennis.

After receiving her B.A. (magna cum laude), Charlene moved on to graduate school at Cornell; she had decided to pursue a career in microbiology. She worked very hard and did extremely well, and by the time she had her master's degree, Charlene was able to devote herself to her doctorate without the distraction of outside work; increased scholarships and a major federal grant covered all her financial needs.

Charlene married a fellow graduate student, a physicist from New York. After receiving their Ph.D.'s, they moved to Seattle, where she became a teaching assistant at the University of Washington and her husband found a research position with an aerospace company.

Their life together is very pleasant. The house they bought

is perfectly suited to their zest for restoration. Their neighbors are mostly young professionals. On one side lives the assistant city budget director and his wife, a law student; on the other, a systems analyst. The houses are old, but the occupants are new. Few of them were born in Seattle and most, like Charlene and her husband, are very recent arrivals. They have their newness in common; initially it was the basis for their friendships. There is no need for them to go elsewhere for companionship. The social life of the neighborhood is largely self-contained.

No one is rich, but almost all are better off than were their parents. Many households have two professional incomes. They can afford new furniture—not, perhaps, the opulent selections of the decorator magazines but surely good pieces. They enjoy having dinner in one another's homes; there is candlelight and wine—and much sharing of recipes for, say, ratatouille or an exotic curry. While they like to eat in restaurants occasionally, they scorn the most expensive of these as "tourist traps" and hunt with competitive zeal for some "authentic" fare—Syrian, Greek, Thai, or Japanese. Their quest is precisely the opposite of Chicago columnist Mike Royko's advice to "stick to restaurants of an ethnic group large enough to have two aldermen." Their taste in clothing favors authenticity, too; some resemble prairie gentry of the last century. And there is enough disposable income to indulge a flowering of interests: foreign films, local crafts, concerts, travel.

Sometimes when Charlene looks at her young son, Josh, she can't help comparing his upbringing to her own. She is proud of the differences but also a little resentful. It isn't so much the material things—they are raising Josh not to think in such terms—but more a question of atmosphere. His childhood seems so much more serene than hers. There is no worry about money and there is unlimited opportunity. The future is secure.

Charlene does not want anything in her life to change. She is very content with things as they are—as they are for her and her family. She knows that things will get even better with the passing of years, that there will be a gradual increase in the household income as both professionals increase their seniority. She wants nothing to disrupt her good life and her plans for Josh's future. She does not want large outside forces to alter in any way her family's steady destiny. She wants to be left alone.

Charlene feels that she has earned her better way of life, that she has risen to her natural level, to the place where she belongs. The same is true of her husband and many of their friends, some of whom left behind backgrounds that they too regard with the same embarrassment as she does her own. She is grateful to have escaped a world that was devoid of verve or culture, in which no one had heard of Bach or Bartok, cocquilles or quiches, Amnesty International or the geodesic dome, or even Adidas or Marimekko.

She is grateful, but to whom? To what? What was it that had wafted her to such improved circumstances? It must have been her own ability that enlightened people had arranged to recognize and reward. The same is true for her friends. They have achieved what they deserve.

Gratitude breeds loyalty. How can Charlene feel loyalty to values and roots she has rejected? How can she avoid a strong allegiance to the new way of life that she has won with her own mind? And if her friends and neighbors hold a point of view, how can she doubt the superiority of that view, since their own superiority is evidenced by what they have achieved.

Charlene is a member of the New Elite and has much in common with other members of her class. She shares with them not only certain taste in clothes and books and films but the same attitude. They reject the past. They disdain tradition. They believe in themselves. Like everyone else, their view of society, based on their own experience, reflects their own interest.

Edward is very affluent, and this sets him apart from many other Left Behinds. He is quite intelligent, too; his IQ is actually higher than Charlene's. Yet he could never be a member of the New Elite, and it is instructive to see why.

Edward grew up in Mankato, Minnesota, a prosperous town

of thirty thousand. His father—and *his* father before him—was a partner in the town's leading law firm. It represented the largest local bank, two of the three biggest businesses in the area, and more than its share of wealthy farmers. Edward's father was one of the leading citizens in Mankato. He served on many boards, both business and civic, and he had been president of the local country club. Everyone knew who he was.

Edward grew up very much aware of his family's place in the scheme of things. Each day brought new reminders of who he was. The mention of his surname produced a knowing look and smiles. He saw respect in the eyes of the parents of his friends. His teachers were very friendly.

Mankato is not that large a town. Many families have been there for several generations. Everyone seems to know everyone else. There is no private secular school in the town, so the sons and daughters of the rich and poor are educated together. This commingling did not detract from Edward's sense of his family's place; it strengthened it. He felt himself part of a community and knew very well his own role in it.

Edward had a very happy youth. His easy manner and athletic skill assured his popularity. He was bright, and his parents had instilled in him the habit of diligence. Despite football and tennis and the captaincy of the school golf team, he was able to finish near the top of his high school class. He had no trouble being accepted by Dartmouth, which his father had attended before him.

Edward's college years were a very pleasant extension of the life he had always known. Many of his classmates were from backgrounds similar to his. There were sports and girls and modest academic success. His fraternity was one of the best.

It never seriously occurred to Edward to seek his fortune outside of Mankato. He considered himself part of a very acceptable tradition. After graduation (cum laude) he enrolled in the University of Minnesota law school. His father had been there, too, and it was supposedly very helpful to study law along with so many other future colleagues in the state bar.

Edward worked much harder in law school than he had in

college, and at the end of his first year was asked to join the Law Review. His success was motivated by pride, not necessity. Regardless of where he finished in his class, a desk would be waiting for him in the family firm. He regarded this as an obligation to do well.

In the summer following his second year of law school, Edward married a young woman from Mankato whom he had known all his life. She had been at Smith, and he had dated her exclusively since his junior year. Her father owned a processing plant, and their parents were good friends.

The practice of law is the same in Mankato as anywhere else, except that Edward is able to walk home for lunch. He works very hard, with commendable results, but there is time for golf and active memberships in the chamber of commerce, the church, and the Republican party. He helped lead the campaign to fund some sculpture for the town plaza.

Edward's home is near his parents', of which it is a smaller, newer version. Ostentation is avoided in their set, but Edward's wife has considerable flair and the leisure to indulge it. Theirs is a very comfortable life: dinners at the club and frequent trips to Minneapolis to see old friends and attend plays. They stay at home more often now that they have a son, Edward, Jr.

It is impossible to think of Edward as a member of the New Elite, because it is impossible that he would think of himself as a member. That's the whole point. It's a matter of self-selection.

Edward knows that he is intelligent, of course. That had been verified by tests and grades and in the competitive practice of law. Yet this has very little to do with the way he sees himself. Privately, he harbors feelings of superiority, but these are quite divorced from any IQ scores. Other factors played major roles in shaping his strong sense of identity. He acknowledges his own ability but certainly doesn't see himself as a member of a class based on academic achievement. Instead, he sees himself as a local aristocrat, one whose family has always been among those who ran the town. He views himself, also, as a lawyer, as the literal heir to the standards of a profession. He sees himself as a Dartmouth man. He sees himself as a Republican. He sees himself as a golfer. If he had done less well in school—or if he'd done even better—his life and his values would not have been significantly altered. He feels he owes his comfortable status in life not so much to his measurable intelligence as to other things: a social order, an economic system, a society that rewards certain traits as well as testable skills. He is grateful to the traditional scheme of things.

The examples of Charlene and Edward were chosen to illustrate certain characteristics. Neither should be considered a prototype. It is not necessary to be as well-educated as Charlene to be a member of the New Elite; many of its members have undistinguished and limited academic records. But if they hold jobs that require verbal or technical skills, and if they identify principally with similar types, then their class membership could be well established—even if their real intelligence is not. Edward is atypical of the Left Behinds because of his income and education, but he does represent the loyalty to roots and traditon that qualifies him for classification as a Left Behind—or, rather, that disqualifies him for the New Elite.

The point of the examples in this: Membership in the New Elite is not determined· so much by either IQ or education as it is by the rejection of traditional values. Most important, it is a matter of self-identification, a matter of self-inclusion in a class. If one's primary identity is with the new class of educated professionals, and if one shares its values (which are based on a rejection of traditional values), then one is a member of the New Elite.

In a sense, IQ is not very important at all. *Class identity and loyalty are what really matter.* The significance of measured intelligence is that it propels many into the class in the first place and serves to justify the class self-image and demands later on.

You don't have to be very bright to hold many of the jobs that lead to the rather uniform income range and life-style of the New Elite. In this sense, Charlene is an imperfect example because she has achieved real academic distinction and is actually employed as a scholar. Most members of the New Elite fall far short of her ability or attainments. A researcher for a state legislature, a public information officer of a corporation, a wide range of administrators, planners, copywriters, counselors, consultants, analysts, technicians, and hundreds of thousands of workers at middle-level jobs and of middling ability are members of the New Elite, too. Many of them are not very gifted, cultivated, or exceptional in any sense, but they tend to have at least a college education and ostensible skills sufficient to hold down a vast and increasing number of jobs in a society where blue-collar workers are now actually a minority. They do not work with their hands. Their jobs, many of them routine, are often (but not always) more remunerative than physical labor. They do not achieve huge rewards and they are seldom rich, but their incomes permit comforts and attitudes sufficient to ensure a standard of living distinct from that of the traditional labor force.

This standard of living is pleasant enough to permit a sense of achievement and well-being. To most members of the New Elite, it represents an improvement over the environment in which they were raised. It allows them to think of themselves as members of a somewhat privileged class. It's enough to separate themselves (in their own view) from the great mass of people whom they feel they've left behind.

No matter how mediocre their talent or mundane their jobs, their sense of superiority is supported because they receive somewhat more money and status than many others. Our society rewards their testable skills and therefore causes them to value their own skills even more highly. They identify with others of similar skills and jobs and rewards. A sense of class identity emerges. This is the first step.

The emphasis on intelligence comes later—after the class allegiance has been formed, at which time it becomes very important. Intelligence is used to distinguish the New Elite from ordinary workers who make nearly as much money and from businessmen who make much more. It's used to confer particular status on a group that can never reach the highest income brackets. Those whose primary identity is with this new class quite naturally place great store on the value of measured intelligence—supposedly the key to their improved way of life. By emphasizing its origins, the class defines itself as unique and gains credence for its insistence on a special role.

The formation of a large class of educated professionals was not possible until very recently. Several preconditions had to be met: a remarkable increase in certain kinds of jobs; an industrial society so far advanced that its economy could justify a major allocation of resources to management, research, and explication; many new jobs that could be filled not merely by members of a preexistent economic or social elite but by those to whom this new employment represented an improved standard of living with which they would want to identify, rather than seeing it as the extension of a previous caste; a social arrangement that identified the testable skills of its citizens, and which made it inevitable that most of those with certain skills would identify with—and marry—one another; a clustering, a segregation, of these skilled workers by neighborhood, by employment, by life-style, and, above all, by family unit. Finally, there had to be the sense—necessary to the formation of any class—that what these people had in common could be handed down to their succeeding generations.

All of these conditions have been met. The new class has been formed. Its members number in the millions. They do not include everyone with the requisite testable ability. David Rockefeller has a Ph.D. in economics, but one can surmise that his class identify is with an old financial elite. A devoutly Orthodox Jewish physicist may identify so strongly with his coreligionists that his sense of identity is unrelated to his profession. A doctor who is the son of a farmer may continue to think of himself in terms of his rural roots. The very brightest people in society—the most extraordinarily creative in their fields—may think of themselves as so superior to their co-workers that no sense of class can possibly arise.

Almost everyone sees the world in terms of Us and Them. Accordingly, Albert Einstein could not have been a member of the New Elite, for despite his remarkable intellectual gifts, he seems to have regarded his fellow humans as Us. Neither his writings nor his manner suggest that he saw himself as a member of any class, though he had a strong sense of identity with other scientists and fellow Jews. There is no evidence that he saw his genius at physics as testament to a right to determine social policy for others.

Pablo Picasso was not a member of the New Elite. He saw himself as an artist, and surely the question of IQ was irrelevant to what he felt himself to be. He was Picasso, and that was enough.

Henry Kissinger is not a member of the New Elite, though his academic credentials are exemplary. In his world, success is certified by power, not grades. His celebrated ego pertains to himself and not to any class.

Alexander the Great or Frederick the Great or William Pitt or Talleyrand or Bismark or Disraeli might have considered themselves superior in ability to their contemporaries and more deserving than anyone else to govern human lives. But each saw *himself* this way. None saw a distinct class of the intellectually able to whom the reins of government belonged by right. Indeed, each of these rulers did feel some class loyalty, but the object of that loyalty was to hereditary social classes whose intellectual superiority was neither demonstrable nor relevant.

The examples above illustrate the point that too much ability (or success) may preclude a sense of belonging to any class, even that of an intellectual elite. The more confident and successful a person, the more likely it is that he draws his self-esteem from his own achievements, not from the collective accomplishments of others like himself.

Those whose sense of success is based on identification with a group are far more likely to be members of the New Elite. These people *define themselves* as members of that class and their definition of themselves affects their definition of everyone else. It's the window through which they see the world.

It is easiest to view the world through only one window if most of the others have been boarded up. The degree to which one's measured intelligence becomes the basis of his or her self-identity depends on the extent to which other loyalties or roots are rejected. As a general rule, the less reliance on background or roots, the greater the likelihood of self-inclusion in the New Elite. A clean slate invites new scribblings.

Millions of Americans today begin their adult lives with furious erasure. In this regard, the example of Charlene is typical of many well-educated young people who have deliberately sought to divorce the past from their present. In an age of marked social and economic mobility, of the disintegration of neighborhoods, of quick and frequent changes in the places people live, of the erosion of the most basic "root" institutions—family and church—it is for an increasing number of people no longer even a question of rejecting roots: it is a matter of never having acquired roots in the first place. If people derive their identity from the positions to which their measured intelligence has taken them, it is perhaps because there are few alternative sources from which they can define that identity at all.

So, the first step is a class awareness. The next is to attach significance to that class—to find and proclaim those things that make it special. This is a natural progression: everyone seeks to extol the group to which he or she belongs. Farmers stress the virtues of the rural ethic. Aristocrats speak of breeding. Members of every group seek to locate the most commendable trait its members share, then emphasize this one aspect of identity to enhance the status of the group and through it their own self-esteem.

With the New Elite, the commendable trait is intelligence. Not for them the argument that city planners are better than plumbers or boasting about one's income. They prefer to emphasize the source of their bounty: measured intelligence.

Jobs, income, life-style, and taste were made possible for some individuals because they scored well on tests. (Even those who gained their comfortable livelihoods through nepotism or luck believe this.) This is the focus of the New Elite pride. They like to emphasize not what they have but how they got it. They see themselves as the only class whose position was earned by scientific measurement.

But measurement of what? The New Elite does not doubt the answer: measurement of intelligence, of general ability. It feels that its members have been objectively selected as the "best" in society, that their general intelligence has been "proven" beyond a doubt. They accept as a given that their clear superiority in the making of all decisions has been unarguably established.

This stems from a misunderstanding of what is measured by intelligence tests. There has long been a widely-held (but never verified) conclusion that there is a single unit known as "general intelligence," and that this can be measured. Intelligence tests can be said to be "verifiable"; i.e., when one excludes the effects of cultural disadvantage, one can, by correlation with other tests or achievements, demonstrate that IQ tests on the whole provide a roughly accurate tool of measurement. But again, measurement of what? That is the central question, and it has never been precisely answered. In fact, it has seldom even been asked. IQ tests *seem* to measure certain abilities that society rewards. When they score well on those tests, some individuals are rewarded by society. Even assuming that this inherent circularity proves the accuracy of the test, it says nothing at all about the test's *object*: we still don't know what it is that is being measured. It has been said in jest that the only thing an IQ examination really tests is the ability to do well on an IQ examination.

The New Elite does not find that very amusing. They believe that there is such a thing as "general intelligence," that it can and has been measured, and that those with high scores are generally better able to make correct decisions than those with lower scores. This is less a conclusion than an attitude. It is certainly an assumption seldom questioned by those whose role it enhances. It is easier to understand than to justify such uncritical acceptance. Personal experience has verified the test results for most members of the New Elite. Charlene was told by a test score that she would get better grades in graduate school than almost any of her classmates, which she did. Charlene's husband competed for a very good job against four or five other applicants whose grades were not so high as his own. It would be more natural (though not more reasonable) for him to assume that he was the best qualified applicant than it would be to infer that the decision to hire was based on the only available index of ability, and that he happened to excel on that one index. In their own lives, members of the New Elite have observed that test scores accurately predicted that certain rewards would follow from certain scores. The recipients of those rewards are the least likely to question the appropriateness of the procedures by which they gained them. Because the tests are "accurate" in correlating scores with rewards, they are seen as accurate in equating scores with ability.

Equally significant is the perceived value of quantified "proof." People learn that some things can be proven objectively. It can be proven, for example, that water is heavier than oil. It can be accurately predicted that one out of every seven persons born will be left-handed. Educated people have been taught that certitude rests on quantification. If something can be quantified, it can be proved or predicted. It is now widely assumed that intelligence has been quantified. Precise numbers are applied to each variant response to standardized tests. This quantification has had uncritical acceptance, as if the use of numbers alone precluded argument. Numbers are seen as absolute: one can demonstrate absolutely that one column of numbers represents a higher total than another. The problem with all of this rests in the value of the numbers themselves. Something can be quantitatively "verified" even if the numbers have been arbitrarily assigned. The real test should be whether the numbers themselves are based on objective reality. This test can be met, say, in ascertaining the weight of water. We can ascribe a numerical weight to a liter of water, and that weight can be verified by comparison with other liquids. The numerical weights assigned to oil and water can be verified by placing equal units of each on opposite sides of a scale. By this comparison the numbers (weights) assigned to each can be objectively based on reality. This is not the case with IQ scores. One can compare those with high scores to those with low and demonstrate that the former group will make more money, receive higher grades, gain higher status, and so forth. But jobs and grades have no absolute meaning in themselves; they represent certain values and skills that society has chosen to reward. They may be the rewards only for certain aspects of intelligence. There is no way yet devised by which the concept of "general intelligence" can be objectively based on reality. The assignment of numbers to intelligence does not alter this fact; it obscures it. Quantification does not consist wholly in what use we make of numbers; it depends as well on the inherent value of the numbers. The use of numbers in itself does not establish that value. Such value must be demonstrated to be based on reality; with regard to general intelligence, this has not been done.

But the numbers are there, and because they are numbers they are taken as objective proof. Most other things with accepted numerical value have been legitimately quantified, and so it is unthinkingly assumed that IQ scores have been, too. People accept the fact that someone with an IQ score of 140 is "smarter" than someone with a score of 110, just as they accept a day when the temperature is ninety degrees as warmer than a day when the temperature is only sixty-five; and a car that goes ninety miles an hour as faster than a car that cannot exceed sixty-five. Heat and speed can be related to reality; so far, general intelligence cannot. In all these cases we can relate the various numbers to one another with equal precision. With heat and speed we know what the numbers *mean*; but while we know how to use the numbers that are supposed to indicate intelligence, we do not know what they mean. We do not really know that someone is smarter than someone else in the same way that we know something to be warmer or faster than its comparison.

The New Elite has missed this point. Its members feel not only that their general intelligence is superior to everyone else's but that this can be objectively demonstrated. The New Elite derives the "proof" of its superiority from numbers that have been arbitrarily assigned. This is the heart of the problem. It presents the basic danger posed to society by the New Elite. It justifies to the New Elite both the need and the right to govern, the right to make the basic societal decisions that determine the conditions under which everyone lives.

The assumption of the right to govern follows logically from the mistaken view that general intelligence can be accurately measured. Most of the great issues facing society are not resolvable by objective "proof." One can argue eloquently the merits of one form of taxation over another, or the desirability of some foreign intervention, or of a certain distribution of wealth. A society may become convinced that prostitution should be legalized or that God exists. But these things cannot be proved objectively by a process so certain that it is followed by a cessation of debate. It is precisely because one cannot "prove" the superiority of one policy over another that many societies permit their resolution through the processes of majority rule. The welter of argument and the weighing of values are submitted to the people and it is hoped that the policy they select will be better tailored for society's needs than the alternatives. By definition, that policy will enjoy majority support and thus contribute to the general stability of society. It is conceded that sometimes the majority will select the wrong policy, but that is a calculated risk; there seems no better way.

But the New Elite thinks it has a better way. Its members don't deny that the great policy questions of the day cannot be decided by some objective formula that vitiates all doubt. They concede that one cannot "prove" that income should be distributed in a certain way, or that prostitution should be legalized. After all, such things are not subject to quantifiable proof. But something else is: their own superiority. This, they feel, can be and has been measured as certainly as the weight of water, and as subject to numerical gradation as the variances of heat and speed.

Policy itself may not be subject to such objective exactitude, but "general intelligence" is. And, it follows, if one knows precisely who the "smartest" people are, then that is enough for the formulation of public policy. That policy should be decided by the ablest people. Formerly, they feel, the ablest had not been identified; they were scattered throughout the general population. The only way to solicit their views was to poll the entire population. But now those days are over. The ablest members of society are known and numbered. If they agree on a matter of policy, then it must be right.

Other elites have wanted their views to prevail, but only the New Elite believes that its views must prevail because the holders of those views are demonstrably superior to the rest of society. If one believes that all this is scientifically certain, then one believes that the views of the New Elite should prevail on all occasions and at any cost. No tactic is unjustified if it helps enshrine the views of those who know best. Majoritarian institutions are seen as barriers that must be breached, anachronisms from a time before the ablest citizens could be identified. To bypass those institutions, to subvert and replace them, is regarded as logical and desirable, the natural deployment of new knowledge. The right of the New Elite to prevail over the majority seems (to its members) as inevitable as the replacement of candle power by electricity—as inevitable as any other scientific advance. And, just as the views of the "smartest" must be best for society, so the objections of the rest of society can be discounted because that majority is by definition less able than its objectively selected elite. The emphasis is no longer on which policies are best, but rather on who is best able to decide which policies are best. The search for peers has replaced the discussion of issues in current political activity. The point of governance is not what should be done but who should do it.

This new perception stems not only from the assumption that general intelligence can be tested; it arises from the corollary assumption that public policy can be formulated by reason alone. Implicitly, in deciding policy matters, the New Elite regards rationality as vastly more important than experience. The coming political battles between the New Elite and the Left Behinds are in large part a contest between the relative roles of reason and experience. Majoritarianism is the obvious preference of those who value the role of experience in the construction of public policy. If experience best defines the needs and hopes of each individual, then the aggregate experience of all people should provide the basis and direction of public policy. This is what Justice Holmes meant when he wrote that "a page of history is worth a volume of logic." But to the New Elite the reverse is true. To them, logic is everything in human affairs, and history merely the sordid chronicle of its absence. Experience may have defined what people want, but reason alone can determine what they *should* want.

Their fundamental objection to experience is that everyone has had it. Everyone has faced the effects of taxation and big government and social change and the most basic societal experience of all, the process of getting along with other people. To rely on experience is to rely on majority rule.

And there is no formula, no quantitative means, for proving that one person's experience is more meaningful than that of another. One is forced to regard all people as equal. With rationality, however, such leveling can be avoided. It is possible to assert that some people can reason more capably than others. Numbers can and have been assigned to the relative capacity to ratiocinate. Those with the highest numbers tend to see the clear superiority of reason over experience in the conduct of public affairs. They become more convinced than ever that success in government depends not so much on choosing correct policy but on identifying those select individuals who should be entrusted with the making of that policy.

This is not a matter of metaphysics. The experience-versus-reason polarity, the temporary ascendancy of one viewpoint over the other, has the most direct and dramatic effects on society. In the 1960s, for example, a group of New Elitists, of whom McGeorge Bundy may serve as the perfect example, succeeded in altering the direction of American foreign policy. By the rarified application of reason alone, Bundy decided that the United States should become militarily involved in Vietnam. His reasoning was elaborate and profound, and it relied in part on innovative concepts such as a "domino theory" of intensifying loss that could be prevented only by the immediate deployment to South Vietnam of American troops and equipment. Against this glittering analytical construct much simpler men, including many military officers, could argue only from experience, which suggested that land wars in Asia waged from the West had always ended in failure. Bundy's reasoning prevailed, and the rest is history—for those who still believe that history is relevant.

The significant fact is that Bundy's views prevailed. His policy was adopted partly because his brilliance was indisputable. His intellectual credentials were breathtaking. Summa cum laude at Groton, the first Yale student to get three perfect scores on his college entrance exams, dean of Harvard College at thirty-four, eloquent in discourse and devastating in debate, his intellectual superiority was patently obvious. It surely impressed and reassured the president whom he served, Lyndon Johnson, a man not noted for modesty but curiously insecure in the supposedly arcane realm of foreign policy and all too aware, despite his very considerable gifts, of the contrast between the Ivy League laurels of his advisors and his own background at Southwest Texas State. The critical anecdote that reveals Johnson's attitude is recounted in David Halberstam's *The Best and the Brightest*. Halberstam relates that Johnson, as vice-president, attended the first meeting of the Kennedy cabinet and was overwhelmed by the credentials of its members. "Stunned by their glamour and intellect, he had rushed back to tell [House Speaker Sam] Rayburn, his great and crafty mentor, about them, how brilliant each was, that fellow Bundy from Harvard, Rusk from Rockefeller, McNamara from Ford. On he went, naming them all. 'Well, Lyndon, you may be right and they may be every bit as intelligent as you say,' said Rayburn, 'but I'd feel a whole lot better about them if just one of them had run for sheriff once.'"

It is instructive that the most thorough account of the decisions that led to the disaster in Vietnam is titled *The Best and the Brightest*. Its author concluded that "if those years had any central theme, if there was anything that bound the men, their followers and subordinates together, it was the belief that sheer intelligence and rationality could answer and solve anything."

It all boils down to this: The New Elite believes that reason alone can solve any problem, and that its members are the best reasoners. Therefore, they think, the New Elite knows best—about everything. In fact, they conclude, the New Elite *is* the best; not exactly the "best and the brightest" but quantifiably the brightest and therefore the best. They are certain of their superiority and just as certain that it can and has been objectively "proven."

There is a third step to membership in the New Elite: the demand for power. The New Elite feels that if one group is able to make the best decisions, then its decisions should be followed. If one group knows best, it should govern; its will alone should prevail. They consider the need for majority sanction outmoded, a leftover from the days before ability could be precisely measured. From now on, they feel, the New Elite alone should determine the course of society, should be able to make the decisions for everybody else. To believe this is, of course, to reject the requirement of majority rule. That requirement and the structure and tradition that support it must be avoided and evaded until they are no longer meaningful. In politics, this undermining of majority rule is already very advanced and the damage is extensive. The New Elite has already transformed and weakened much of our political system, and they have made vast inroads toward the dominance of our society. The goal of this dominance is not the enactment of any particular ideology but the enthronement of certain personnel. It is rule by the New Elite for its own sake. The New Elite is so certain of its superiority that its sole political objective is to see its members placed in positions of power so that all future governance will be safeguarded. It seeks to recognize its own and guarantee to them the right to govern all.

This is not always easy. Recognizing one another requires some skill. It can even be a formidable task. People can't walk up to strangers and ask what their L.S.A.T. scores were; even if they could, test scores and grades alone are very fallible guides to recognition of the New Elite. What the New Elite seeks is not really those of high intelligence; that category is too broad. Instead, the search is for allies. Intelligence is the putative attribute that gives credence to the claims of the class, but the class itself is what really matters to its members, and the signs of that class allegiance are the true beacons of its search.

Some of those signs are easier to spot than others. As mentioned earlier, a reliable clue is the way in which people earn their living. Occupation is considered a good index of membership in the New Elite. Certain kinds of jobs suggest the probability of class allegiance. Any work that requires "objectively" tested ability confers the new class status.

Life is much simpler when one believes all this. A person's "intelligence" may be deduced from the position in society that that person has attained. One need only apply the New Elite's threshold test. Once that test has been met, eligibility then depends on inward things: attitude, identity, the level of rejection of one's roots.

Membership is definitely not a question of how much money someone has. The membership test for the New Elite is only incidentally economic. In fact, too much money may serve as a disqualifier—and not only in the case of inherited wealth. For example, Texas oil millionaires are never seen as members of the New Elite by those who are. An associate professor of history makes a good deal less money than the president of a department store, yet the former may meet the achievement test easily while the burden of proof may hang heavily on the latter. The New Elite recognizes intelligence partly in terms of success, but it has its own strict notions as to what constitutes the proper success—that based on testable skills. Academia and the professions provide the most obvious examples. The wrong kind of achievement, the great disqualifier for the New Elite status, is success based on the marketplace rather than on the test score.

The marketplace is the forum of economic majoritarianism. Success there depends on appealing to the largest number of people. Most small businessmen are therefore economic majoritarians. Their rewards are not awarded as the result of a certain score but are won in the marketplace. The same is true for merchants, manufacturers, salesmen, and for some people in advertising. These fields are regarded with great suspicion by the New Elite. The owner of a chain of hardware stores might conceivably be accepted as a member, but only after considerable demonstration that his true values were quite different from those of his fellow merchants. (It's unlikely that they would be; those who succeed in the marketplace have the best reason to believe in the good sense of the general public.)

It is noteworthy that these careful distinctions of work and wealth are almost unrelated to the subject of IQ. The self-made businessman might very well be more intelligent than the associate professor of biology, and his superiority might be independently evidenced even by test scores and college grades. This is obviously true in a great many such comparisons—perhaps in most—but it is of no matter to those who see themselves as the New Elite. Their loyalty is to the categorical manifestations of testable meritocracy, and not to individual examples of intelligence itself. Theirs is a class loyalty. They resent, perhaps most of all, the obviously gifted businessman because his success is an evasion, or even a denial, of their basic loyalty, which is the source of their own identity. By prospering in the marketplace, to a degree greater than they can achieve as his employees, he causes others to participate in that majoritarian forum and to see it as a valid determinant of where ability truly lies.

The relation of status to jobs is very complicated. The distinctions maintained by the New Elite are various and subtle. For example, while the practice of law ranks highly with the New Elite, there are gradations. An attorney who practices corporate law is more likely to be seen as a peer than is a trial lawyer. While it is impossible to demonstrate that either of these specialties requires more general intelligence than the other, it is generally thought that the skills of the former are more nearly related to testable qualities such as analytical ability or the capacity to analogize. The trial lawyer may well possess these abilities to the same degree, but they necessarily are directed toward persuasion of a jury, and success depends on winning the minds and emotions of a randomly selected panel of citizens. Such direct interaction with the general public vitiates the trial lawyer's credentials in comparison with other members of the bar who work with paper, and not people. Theirs is considered a loftier pursuit, the results of which depend on objective criteria, such as reasoning and deduction. It is assumed that success won by the consensus of a jury is inherently less defensible.

This sort of distinction permeates the whole spectrum of employment. As described earlier, the basic New Elite test for the ranking of job status appears to be based on how removed a person's work is from ratification by the public. A scientist's progress can be measured by objective, neutral principles; their need not be a human factor at all. Bankers, on the other hand, occupy a somewhat perilous place in the New Elite hierarchy. It is conceded that they deal rationally with the allotment of funds and the analysis of projects, but what cannot be overlooked is that much of their work involves the granting of loans, which depend in part on adroit assessment of human nature. Investments, no less than loans, are ultimately related to success in the marketplace, to appeals for public favor. This taint is noted, regardless of how well-educated and rational a banker may be, or how much distance from the masses he maintains in his daily conduct. In addition, there is the overpowering fact that bankers believe in the power of money. Power to the New Elite is a task awarded to the measurably able. Dealing with, and affirming, the connection of power with wealth is antithetical to their concept of how the world should really work.

There is no formal chart that ranks the New Elite status of each job. And even if there were, people don't casually describe what they do with enough specificity to permit exact placement on such a chart. In any event, job description alone can't qualify one for the New Elite, any more than does a certain income or an IQ score. This kind of information is helpful but not dispositive. Attitude is what is all-important; knowing someone's educational background, job, and salary are helpful only because they suggest what that person's attitude might be.

That's why style is of particular importance. The life-style of the New Elite is the most reliable guide to its members' mutual recognition. Clothes and cars and food and countless nuances of speech and decoration proffer all the clues in the search for shared identity. This is an area of manifold subtlety, and it is often impossible to distinguish the New Elite life-style from that of most members of the upper-middle class. But there *are* two factors that distinguish the New Elite: the stringent avoidance of any item or conduct that enjoys wide public popularity and the deliberate adoption of life-styles that are at variance with one's own roots.

Large cars, steak and potatoes, (domestic) beer, network television, bowling, and church affiliation are such common preferences as to be rejected by the New Elite. Lawyer A may have attended the same schools and received the same high grades as lawyer B. Their professional duties and salaries are identical and each earns $70,000 per year. Yet their life-styles identify lawyer A as a member of the New Elite and lawyer B as merely a professional man with a good income. Lawyer B lives in a large new house in an affluent suburb. His home is filled with appliances and gadgets, and he owns two cars, both large and both American. In these matters he has attempted not to reject the standard aspirations of American society but to amplify them. Lawyer A's house is nearly one hundred years old, and the considerable sums he lavished on it were directed to restoring as much of its original style as possible. In a society in which the new and modern and gleaming are popular standards of domestic ambiance, an older home, redolent of a past era, is divergent enough to appeal to the New Elite. Lawyer A removed all the wall-to-wall carpeting that came with his house and covered the oak floor sparingly with throw rugs. This was not entirely an aesthetic decision. In the middle-class household in which lawyer

A was raised, wall-to-wall carpeting was considered highly desirable, a mark of affluence and status. Lawyer A, consciously or not, is rejecting a value of his parents and thereby displaying the attitude of the New Elite. Lawyer B has wall-to-wall carpeting—all wool. His parents' carpeting was synthetic. He is not rejecting his parents' values but trying to exhibit a greater attainment of the things that they valued.

There's no one thing that makes all the difference—be it carpeting, clothes, or manner of speech. But all the little things together constitute a style, changeable, changing, imprecise at best as a key to certain ranking but still by far the most available source of information by which the New Elite can surmise who really belongs. Each stylistic detail works to affirm or deny the basic definition of the New Elite.

That definition has several components, of which the easiest to convey through style are high measured intelligence and the rejection of roots and tradition. With regard to the former, intelligence itself is less easily communicated than is the evidence of higher education. It is helpful to know what degrees one has obtained, and from which institutions. While this information is seldom blurted out with introductions, the general impression of one's educational attainments can be conveyed in numerous ways, through vocabulary and expression, through the dropping of phrases and allusions to certain topics, titles, and facts. Clothing, and even hair styles, the adornments of one's person and one's home, a stated preference in films or restaurants, are imperfect but frequent inklings of the influence of academia.

While it is not so difficult to give the impression that one is well-educated, the New Elite must simultaneously display a rejection of roots. This complicates the question of identity by style because the two things may even be at variance with each other. This has become increasingly true as higher education has become widely accessible. Millions of Americans earn diplomas each year, an experience so commonplace that now the ultimate rejection of middle-class values is the decision not to receive a college degree. Some who have chosen this negative option are the ultimate members of the New Elite. The bright children of comfortable backgrounds who scorn both higher education and careers are not really abandoning their identity with the new class, they are affirming it. They may choose to wear overalls instead of tweed, to work with their hands on communes or at kilns, to reject rationality itself and retreat into mysticism or drugs. In such cases the denial of grades or money or professional status or reason is a denial of middle-class values, not of superior status. It's a rejection of roots, not ability. The fact that they don't have to "prove" that ability in school or at jobs shows how confident they are about possessing it. This most recent generation of the New Elite is the most honest in acknowledging what they see as the real source of its identity: heredity. They assume they have inherited from parents (whom they may despise) superior mental ability. This has been confirmed by tests and conveyed to them repeatedly by teachers and family. Theirs is a natural superiority. And since superiority is for them so certain, there is no reason to *do* anything with it. There is no need to prove anything further by achievements. Indeed, to do so would be to suggest that superior status should be earned through deeds instead of simply existing as the natural inheritance of the gifted few.

Most members of the New Elite do not yet share this perception. They see themselves as having been born superior, but for them there's an intermediate step between that perception and its acknowledgement by everyone else. That step is performance, the actual accomplishment of the tasks that society rewards. Perhaps this is a temporary phase in the evolution of the New Elite. Future generations, like the handful of harbingers already among us, may dispense entirely with the requirement of performance. All that will be necessary will be the fact of their measured intelligence. Eventually even that may be regarded as irrelevant; heredity alone may be the ultimate test.

But that is only a speculation. The present disposition of the New Elite is quite different and very clear. Its claims to superiority rest on IQ scores and grades and—most markedly—on the jobs and skills and status and style that have resulted from these measurable indicia. The positions these people have attained are to them the proof that their test scores were right in the first place. What the scores and status together affirm—to them—is a natural superiority in the ability to reason. From there it is but a short step to the next position—the important decisions in this world must be made by them, and them alone—and they have taken that step.

They have been working toward just that goal. In doing so they have tranformed the structure and the scope of our democracy, and they have already destroyed many of the most fundamental underpinnings of our system of majority rule.

CHAPTER 3

THE DEATH OF POLITICS

Everyone knows that something is wrong. People find it hard to articulate, but the feeling is almost universal. There is the sense that nothing works anymore, that events are beyond control, that things just happen. This feeling, unique in our national experience, is probably best described by the word *helplessness*. There is a pervasive fear that we have lost the means to affect our own destiny. This is not purely personal; it has to do with the society as a whole. Our society seems like a rudderless ship: There is no way to steer it nor to alter its course; it is without captain and crew, and we are trapped as its passengers.

This problem is often thought to be political. Surely the most apparent change *is* in the area of politics. Each new poll confirms the worst. People feel alienated from their institutions and the government seems distant, apart. Unresponsiveness above produces apathy below. An alarming number of citizens no longer bother to vote. Candidates for public posts at every level appear interchangeable and mediocre. In fact, so many choices are between the lesser of competing evils that the very concept of choice is now eroded. The level of discourse is dangerously low. There is no focus at all to public issues.

Other times have seemed bad, too, but surely this is different. The conflicts of the past seem preferable to the utter resignation of the present. This may be the quietest crisis in our history; in many ways, however, it is the worst.

Perhaps the most disturbing aspect of this crisis is the failure to pinpoint its cause. In fact, the most frequent explanation one hears is actually just the opposite of the truth. The standard line places all blame on the political process. Yet politics has been the victim, not the cause, of the present problem. We're in the mess we're in because the political process has been abandoned. That process, however imperfect, provided the link between the people and their government, between our hopes and our future, and when that process was rejected, that link was severed. Politics is not killing us; on the contrary, politics is dead.

It isn't only the old politics that's dead, but *all* politics. What was recognizable and workable in our political structure has vanished. Political parties are hollow shells. The lines of communication are down. All the innards of our system of self-government have been disparaged and dismantled. In short, there is no politics anymore.

Its death was not accidental. Someone caused it to happen. The destruction of our political process was executed by those who had the most to gain from its demise: the New Elite. The growth of this new class coincided with, and was responsible for, the decay and expiration of politics as the mechanism for popular consent.

This was necessary in order for the New Elite to expand its power within our society. If the New Elite were to rule, then the majority could not. Those institutions that made it possible for the majority to rule had to be destroyed. Elections, parties, candidates, attitudes—all the apparatus of popular consent had to be changed beyond recognition.

And this is just what had happened. It's what accounts for the panic and confusion that we feel as a people today. Of course, the destruction of our political system is not a deed that could be done openly. It simply would not have been tolerated. So it had to be accomplished by stealth.

No one proposed a law abolishing elections. But some people could—and did—so change the way we do things that elections are deprived of meaning. No one dared seriously to demand an end to political parties. But through radical alteration of both rules and attitudes the parties have nearly ceased to exist. And most preposterous of all would be to decree that people should have no say in their own governance. Yet that is what we've come to—close enough, at any rate, for the loss to be felt all around us, though its causes are not yet obvious.

The causes must be recognized, though, and soon, if there is any hope of reversing what has happened. The cure lies in perception. We have to see what has happened, and why.

The political goal of the New Elite is very simple: the transfer of political power to the New Elite. This has very little to do with issues or with the advancement of any philosophy or cause. It does have to do with who is fit to govern—as decided by the New Elite. Since members of the New Elite feel that intelligence can be measured and that it is now possible to know who the "ablest" members of society are, they see no reason why decisions should be put to the less able (the majority). What they want is to rule by themselves.

Their problem is democracy. We transfer power through free elections in which all adults can vote. By tradition and law, the majority rules. The candidate with the most votes wins.

But who decides who the candidates will be? That is the critical question. Traditionally, the answer has been very simple. Political parties choose the candidates—two parties, sometimes, for a brief while, three. Each nominates a candidate, and the public chooses between them. The two-party nominating system seems as integral to our system of government as the election itself.

To the New Elite, political parties are both the barrier and the opportunity to power, the Maginot Line of majority rule. Parties are a barrier because there are only two of them, so winning an election means attracting a majority of the voters. On the other hand, parties are an opportunity because they provide the only alternatives between which the voters can choose. If one or both of the parties can be captured, alternatives can be dictated to the voters; hence, sanction by the majority has no meaning. If the voters can choose only between the offerings of the New Elite, then the majority no longer rules. The Maginot Line can be breached.

The opportunity has been taken. The effort has been underway for quite some time; though it is not yet completely successful, enormous inroads have been made. The parties are not yet wholly captured, but they are gravely weakened. The barrier to New Elite political control is almost down.

The most serious damage has been inflicted by changes in the rules under which the parties operate. It is difficult to overstate the impact of this tactic. Yet because the subject of rules, particularly those governing a political party, is of very little interest to most citizens, many of the changes have gone unnoticed. The press has directed its vigilance toward candidates and elections; it seldom mentions the inner workings of the parties. As a result, the changes in the rules constitute the great unreported political story of recent times—and one unmatched in our tradition of self-governance. It is a story of the reversal of that tradition, performed covertly and from within. It is a story that concerns both parties, but we shall focus on the Democratic Party, where the rules were more profoundly changed.

The most important rule change was the abolition of winner-take-all. In its place was set up a whole new system of proportional representation. This was accomplished in the name of reform, and to most observers, it seemed like an enlightened step at the time. It is important to note just what time that was.

The year 1968 marked the peak of political protest against the war in Vietnam. In the following years popular support for that cause would grow, but 1968 saw its sharpest political focus. The source of that focus was the Eugene McCarthy campaign. It offered opponents of the war the opportunity for immediate change, peace instead of war. (By 1972, each party was claiming that it could achieve peace more quickly.) The McCarthy campaign was not outside the political process. It was directed toward a very specific political goal—the selection of enough delegates to the Democratic National Convention to win the nomination for Senator McCarthy.

In those days most delegates to a national convention were selected at state conventions. Some states, like New Hampshire, had presidential primaries where the delegates were elected at the polls, but most states—thirty-seven out of fifty—did not. It seems so far away now, but as recently as 1968, national convention delegates generally were chosen by the parties, not the public. State parties chose these delegates in several ways. Some followed a precinct caucus system, where every party member could take part, and others relied on appointment by party or state officials. Some states had primaries that were not binding; they were an index of how the voters felt, but the delegates selected need not reflect those voters' wishes.

These arrangements caused considerable resentment. Sometimes the fervor of the McCarthy movement resulted in a spectacular victory in a state primary, and at first the joy of the activists was intense. But later, when it came time to pick the delegates, that joy turned to rage. In Pennsylvania, for example, McCarthy won the primary overwhelmingly, but nonetheless, many of Pennsylvania's delegates were pledged to Hubert Humphrey. McCarthy supporters saw this as a grave injustice, a rejection of the popular will. What right did a party chairman, or even a state convention, have to disregard hundreds of thousands of ballots? It wasn't fair.

Or was it? Public opinion polls at that time were unanimous in finding that more Democratic voters favored Humphrey than McCarthy. This was sometimes true even with a state where McCarthy received the most primary votes. If the polls were accurate, there could be only one explanation for what was happening: the primaries were not attracting a perfect cross-section of the general electorate. Indeed, this was—and continues to be—the case. There are far fewer voters in a primary than in a general election. And those who vote in a primary tend to be much better educated than the electorate as a whole. Many rank-and-file members don't care to take an active role in selecting their party's nominee, even when they have a preference as to who that person should be. Their abstinence or confusion or laziness—if that's what it is—is not to be commended. But it remains a fact: A great many voters, particularly the least educated, choose not to vote in primaries, and a disproportionate share of the better educated voters do turn out.

It is not surprising, then, that many of those educated voters looked with favor at the primary results. This was to change very greatly, but in 1968, they saw much to recommend the primary system. It seemed to produce the result that they wanted. It became for them the test of what was right. They claimed that primaries represented "the people" because the primaries represented people like themselves. If the party leaders didn't always choose the candidate who had done well in the primaries, then the party leaders were wrong. In fact, the party system was wrong. It would have to be changed.

Before the year was out, the reform movement had begun within the Democratic Party. Its goal was to completely change the way that party operated by drastically changing the rules. In this regard, the reform movement was astonishingly successful.

The most hated rule and the first to be changed was that which permitted winner-take-all. This practice had particularly outraged the McCarthy delegates, and with good reason. Let us say that a state party convention was entitled to select twenty national delegates. At that state convention, 51 percent of those voting favored Humphrey and 49 percent supported McCarthy. Under winner-take-all, the Humphrey forces would elect all twenty delegates. Not eleven, or even fifteen—all twenty. The McCarthy delegates got nothing at all (except in those places where *they* had 51 percent and could take all the delegates). In state after state this happened and, to put it very mildly, the losers did not like it at all. They swore to do away with the hated system, and they came up with something that they thought would work much better.

The reform movement introduced a system of proportional representation in place of winner-take-all. It was simple and very attractive at first. Each side would get its fair share. A group that had, say, one-third of the votes at a state convention would be guaranteed one-third of the delegates to be elected. No one could possibly argue with that.

Very few did. Once the battles of 1968 were over, the party regulars offered surprisingly little resistance to the clamor for reform. They agreed to much that was proposed; it seemed a small price to pay for the return of intraparty peace, and the incessant cries of the media for party reform would at last be stilled. And the reforms didn't seem so bad to most of the regulars. Proportional representation was a mouthful to pronounce, but when all was said and done, what harm could there be in giving each side its fair share?

The harm, it turned out, lay in figuring out exactly what that share would be. This was anything but easy. If each side was to get *exactly* its fair share, very complex procedures would be needed. Formulas would have to be devised. More rules were needed. And if those new rules were good enough for state conventions, they were good enough for county conventions, too, and precinct caucuses, and every gathering, however small, of party people concerned with party business. Every contingency had to be anticipated. A group could never be allowed even one more delegate than its fair share. Exactitude was the goal, and to reach it the rules grew in number, the search for numerical perfection became even more refined. What if a group was entitled to more than six delegates but fewer than seven? The calculators clicked, and the concept of a *half* delegate was born and codified in still more rules.

The best educated voters—lawyers and teachers, those with

verbal skills and advanced degrees—may have understood all these new rules. Many others did not. And so it came to pass that many ordinary party workers grew confused. A county convention composed of farm families who had known one another all their lives found it impossible to sit down together and choose their own representatives. In the past, this had been very easy— an enjoyable way to discharge one's civic duty. Everyone had simply gathered together in a church basement or Farmer's Union Hall and selected the best from among themselves—the hardest workers for the party, the ablest, the most trustworthy to represent the values of the rest. Suddenly it was very different. At the start of every meeting, the first order of business was the reading of the rules, which went on for quite some time. And when it was over, the participants were confused. It all seemed so difficult. You couldn't just vote for your neighbor, you had to go through a lot of procedures first, to guarantee proportionality, to ensure that mathematical justice would be awarded to each side.

And therein lay another problem, more disturbing to the troubled farmers than the incomprehensible rules: Because the rules were set up to give each side its fair share, they required that there *be* sides. You couldn't apportion things fairly if there was nothing to apportion. You couldn't divide things up with justice if no division existed. The rules had been written with division in mind—the great schism of 1968—so they not only reflected division, they required it. You could no longer get together as a unified whole and select your delegates. The rules didn't permit it. You had to choose up sides. A division of the house was required.

But what if nothing divided the farmers gathered in their hall? What if there was no presidential race on which to take sides, no issue like the war to split them into opposing camps? No matter. To give each side its fair share, you had to have more than one side. The rules provided for it.

People being very resourceful, divisions were found. Everyone might agree on the candidates for president and governor and congressman, but if there was disagreement on who to run for county commissioner, there was an opportunity to choose up sides. So minor disagreements within the party became the basis for structural disunity.

Those divisions were not limited to candidates. The rules provided for proportionality with regard to issues as well. People could choose sides on any issue of the day—price supports, a proposed nuclear power plant, wage and price controls, and so on. Each ideological position was entitled to its fair share. And, as with candidates, if no division was at first apparent, one could eventually be found. Local political units whose members agreed on war, peace, taxes, and the draft could be (and were) divided into opposing camps on the question of how many motorboats should be allowed into a nearby wilderness area. The way was paved for single-issue politics.

This produced a profound change in grass-roots politics. The basis of political organization was no longer those things that unified people but that which divided them. Intraparty fights were no longer the exception, they were the rule. And the encouragement of acrimony wasn't the only thing that was taking place; there was now a retreat from the quest for compromise and accomodation. Previously, those who favored a candidate or a cause strove to attract others to their side. This was now unnecessary. Under the new rules, it was difficult for any side to be totally excluded for it was assured of some representation. The need to attract converts in order to survive was gone. With it went the arts of persuasion, the practice of each side giving up something in order to achieve a slate or a platform that all could support. Consensus had disappeared and with it a unified sense of the whole.

That was just fine with members of the New Elite. They had never approved of compromise anyway. Compromise was for those who weren't absolutely certain they were right. If a group feels that it knows better than any other group what is right and what ought to be, why should the purity of that vision be compromised? To do so would be to let all the people in on decisions that their betters could well make for them. In the political arena, compromise is based on the assumption that every citizen has valuable insights which, when pooled produce a stronger result. But when one group is certain of its superiority, it chafes at diluting its platform or accommodating its candidates for a necessity so base as the winning of majority support. That necessity had been abolished by the new rules. Now it was possible to participate in politics without compromising at all. (As a result, parties were deprived of legitimacy with their traditional voters. Candidates who represented a faction, not a party, began to emerge; platforms were written with few planks which seemed aimed at attracting a consensus.) The New Elite had changed politics from a majoritarian forum to a new process in which the majority view could not be represented, nor indeed even found.

The legacy of the new rules was confusion, divisiveness, and an inability to compromise ideological purity. To this was added the introduction of quotas—sometimes de facto—for the selection of delegates by specific categories. The process grew more and more rigid. The meetings lasted longer and longer. The farmers left their county convention near dawn, confused and frustrated. Many vowed never to return.

All of this happened in the name of reform. Fairness had been the ostensible goal. It was more fair, some said, to achieve perfect proportionality in representation. But was it fair to deprive ordinary citizens of a process they could understand? Was it fair to sacrifice comprehensibility to some ideal of mathematical exactitude? Was it fair to preclude a system in which people could work out their differences together? Was it fair to substitute the certainty of faction for the goal of unity? Was it fair to assume that the rights of a political minority could be protected only through the abolition of majority rule?

Fairness had not been the only banner of reform. Openness was a catchword, too. All the new rules were supposed to make things more open. The natural question is: open to whom? The claim, of course, was that politics would be more open to everyone. The facts suggest otherwise. The reformers used the language of popular consent, but the results show a diminution of that consent. There was much talk of drawing in the poor and disadvantaged, but those were precisely the groups who found the new procedures so difficult. A door was opened wider to a place where fewer cared to go. Increasing numbers of people found political participation too difficult to understand, too acrimonious, too divorced from their own concerns. So they stopped participating.

But others were encouraged by the new procedures. Those whose views on candidates had never found broad acceptance were delighted at the guarantee of representation. Those with parliamentary training and verbal skills reveled in the lengthy deliberations. Those whose professional careers did not require awakening at dawn were more amenable to lengthy evening meetings. The New Elite was very pleased with all the changes. Things truly were more open—for them. What had been done in the name of the people was in fact an exclusion of the people; the only group who actually benefited was the New Elite. And as more and more ordinary citizens dropped out of the process in puzzlement or disgust, the role of the New Elite increased. As fewer people participated, the voice of those who stayed was given greater representation. They called it their fair share.

It all happened very swiftly. By 1972, the Democratic Party was able to nominate George McGovern for the presidency. The convention which bestowed on him the nomination of the nation's largest party boasted that it was more open, more representative, more fairly selected than any in our history. Yet never has a candidate of the majority party done so badly at the polls. If indeed the process had become more representative, why did so many millions desert their party's choice and guarantee the election of Richard Nixon? The change in the rules had deprived the Democratic Party of legitimacy with its voters. Neither candidates nor platform were chosen with the goal of winning broad support—and so they did not win it. But it was not merely a candidate who lost. It was the expectation that a party could speak to and for and from a majority of the citizens.

The damage caused by the new rules went even further.

The party's traditional role was abandoned, and there came to be a new and ominous reliance on primary elections. In state after state, elected officials saw their parties controlled by an increasingly narrow base. They saw that the rules had been changed to permit, even encourage, the dominance of activists, of single-issue factions. It was becoming more difficult for these incumbent officials to stay in office. Traditional party support was eroding. Those who were gaining ascendancy within their own parties were more ideologically rigid and less willing to forgive the compromises that public office required. The new party activists were perfectly capable of nominating for president a candidate of such limited appeal that hundreds of those who shared his party label on the ballot were dragged down with him in defeat. Panicked, angry, anxious for survival, these officials thought they had an answer. They would switch to the primary system.

It was like a land rush. Throughout the nation, state legislators moved with precipitate speed to change their local laws and provide for primary elections. The political map of the country was swiftly transformed. Formerly, only a relative handful of states had chosen national convention delegates through primary elections. Within a few years, the frightened legislators had finished their work: the great majority of states had presidential primaries. A very different way of determining who would run for president had been instituted.

The state legislators who brought this about probably felt very proud of their accomplishment—at first. They believed they had served both the public interest and their own with a single stroke. Their own interest was easy to identify. Once the party could no longer select presidential delegates, it was hoped the new activists would no longer be attracted in large numbers to the party. Unfortunately, it didn't turn out quite that way. With the glamorous lure removed, it was the ordinary party members, not the activists, who stayed away from party affairs. One of the few remaining comprehensible party functions had been the choosing of presidential delegates, and now this too was gone.

But the activists remained. State officials had not evaded their scourge.

The public interest was no better served. In establishing primary elections, state officials had boasted that the task of choosing presidential nominees finally would be put in the hands of the people—a victory for democracy. No longer would the voters be faced on Election Day with the dismal task of choosing the lesser evil.

Recent events have mocked this claim. Every poll confirms that with the spread of primaries the public has grown increasingly disenchanted with its choice for the presidency. The phrase, "choosing between the lesser of two evils," has evolved from complaint to fact, the assumed precondition of the quadrennial national ballot. People do not feel that primaries have given them more control; on the contrary, they have never felt so alienated, so incapable of altering their destiny.

This is the big political story of our time, and it is imperative that we understand exactly why it happened. The New Elite did not impose the primary system on us directly, but it did so alter the parties through rule changes that traditional party leaders themselves switched to primaries as an escape. Every political action brings an equal and opposite reaction; the reaction to the rule changes has been just as disastrous to our democracy as the rule changes themselves. The answer to elitism is not anarchy; however, that is precisely the response that we've been saddled with.

If today's primaries aren't anarchy, they're close enough. Democracy requires not only public participation, but continuity, leadership, and structure as well. The people themselves are surely capable of self-governance, but effective self-governance depends on information. There is no way in a pure primary system for the people to inform themselves adequately about the candidates from whom they must choose—not with so many state primaries, anyway, each on the heels of the last. The candidate comes to town for four hectic days of media events and handshaking, after which the people must vote. There are so many candidates, the time is so short, the din so unenlightening, that there's very little basis on which the diligent citizen can make a rational choice. Most voters *are* rational, and so they do the only thing they can. They try desperately to weed out the grosser incompetents from the pack. They know that one of these phantom figures could end up being *president*, the most powerful person in the world. And so they frantically try to figure out who are the most unstable in this pack of office-seekers, their first priority being to eliminate such candidates. They're wary of the gravest dangers: the finger on the button, the head in the sand. Primary voters are forced by circumstance not to look for the best candidate but for the worst. They can learn nothing from the thirty-second commercials or the mob scene in the supermarket parking lot, so they watch attentively for slips or mistakes, any hint that suggests disqualification. If a candidate cries or loses his temper, that's it. There's not enough time for the voters to give him a second chance.

The candidates who do best in the primaries are those who seem most stable. They are not necessarily the brightest, nor the most experienced or thoughtful—just those who appear to be steady. The prize goes to the most unflappable. The situation is perfect for a Jimmy Carter or a Ronald Reagan, men who smile benignly at any question, charge, insult, mishap, or attack; who never seem to get excited about anything at all; and who clearly meet the threshold test of minimal sanity.

It's not a very good way to pick a president. Certainly the public is entitled to something better. The people ought to be able to select a screening committee, not only to weed out the incompetents but to appraise all the candidates—carefully, over an extended period of time. The test should not be limited to a candidate's behavior in a parking lot but how that person performed throughout a public career. A proper screening committee could analyze each candidate's real stands on the issues—not just the phrases tailored for local consumpiton—and relate those stands to some standard of common values. To really do its job, a screening committee should have worked with the candidates for many years and should be able to judge them from the vantage point of shared experience.

There once were such screening committees; they were called political parties. Now they are no more. They've been altered from within, their functions hurriedly switched to a patch-work system of state primaries. It's true that the screening function performed by those parties was a delegated function, but if government can be representative, why can't politics be as well? Consider the alternative.

Groucho Marx once said that he'd never join a club that would take him as a member. There was considerable wisdom in the jest. He was speaking of the necessity for standards, of the desperate need for a screening committee. If you don't like the screening committee, then get a new one; or reform the com-mittee, but don't reform it out of existence. *Someone* has to screen the applicants, and if no one is permitted to do so, then the final election of new members can scarcely have much meaning.

The ultimate irony of the primary system is that it's being used by the New Elite to further discredit political parties. This gall is divided into three parts. First, the political parties were crippled in their capacity to choose candidates that the people wanted. Then, in reaction to this phenomenon, the job of choosing candidates was thrown to the voters under conditions that made that job impossible. The result was the emergence, on a regular basis, of mediocre and unrepresentative candidates. The public grew angry at the choices it was offered. And now, to feed that anger with its favorite scapegoat, the New Elite is ready to place the blame on the political parties. But it won't wash. The reason that things are going so badly is not that the parties have failed, but that they have been prevented from doing their job. It's not politics that's to blame, it's the lack of politics. The Democratic Party didn't put up Jimmy Carter and the Republican Party didn't nominate Ronald Reagan. They were the choice of dozens of primary elections in which the voters had no rational way to make a choice. If the parties hadn't been reformed almost out of ex-istence, if the thousands of party regulars could have chosen from their broad experience, then the Republicans would probably have nominated Howard Baker and the Democrats, Walter Mondale. (The Democrats in 1972 most likely would have chosen Hubert Humphrey and in 1976, Edmund Muskie.) What we have now are candidates with party labels, but they're not the candidates of the parties. They're the candidates of the primaries—which is not at all the same thing as being the candidates of the people. The people were more satisfied when the selection of candidates was made by their political representatives.

It is instructive to note that the parties are blamed for what they have been prevented from doing, for it's a perfect example of how the New Elite works. First, it identifies a majoritarian institution (the political party) that is a barrier to the new class dominance. It then attempts to control that institution (rule changes). When the majoritarian institution becomes so weakened by these changes that it clearly fails in its task of representing the majority will, a populist alternative is developed (the primary system). The alternative is so strongly intended to avoid elite control that most aspects of representative democracy are limited: the people can participate directly but without structure and thus without effect. The performance of this alternative meets with public disapproval (unhappiness with the choice of candidates). Capitalizing on this disapproval, the New Elite heaps more blame on the majoritarian institution that the alternative replaced (the political party), and so further discredits the barrier to its success in a majoritarian society.

There are other examples. In California, political parties became so weak that there was no communicative link between the people and their representatives. As a consequence, neither the governor nor the legislature seemed fully aware of public rage over soaring property taxes. No state action was taken to reduce such taxes, despite a five billion dollar state surplus. Pent-up voter frustration finally exploded with the infamous Proposition 13. This alternative was so crude and heavy-handed that it caused many new problems. Now some citizens would blame those problems on the political system—when party politics could have prevented the crisis in the first place.

All over America, legislators appear to be out of touch with the voters. This is because the political parties have been so gravely weakened. Under a properly working political system, the concerns of most voters would become the basis of party endorsement and the problems of the people would become the agenda of government. With parties virtually out of the picture, however, even the most obvious public concerns are unconveyed. Candidates survive primaries and win election by appealing to enough single-issue groups to garner a majority of the votes. But this is not a true majority—there's no one concern shared by its members. There are a series of small mandates to raise teacher's salaries or ban smoking, but there is no big mandate to get to the problems that everyone must face. So most voters, even those who voted for the winners, don't see that their legislators are working on—or are even aware of—the big issues that truly affect us all. That's why we see a movement in so many states for the use of initiative and referendum—the old and very ineffective populist ploy to avoid the need for government altogether. Were we to reach a stage where nothing remained but three or four big referenda each year, the New Elite surely would proclaim a failure of democracy. Of course, it's not really democracy that's failing but all the half-baked alternatives that arose when our democracy was prevented from working. The New Elite gums things up and then points at its mess to justify further tampering.

It's important to note as well that each step to limit democracy has been made in the name of expanding it. Well aware that our tradition of majority rule still commands affection and respect, the New Elite adapts its tactics to that awareness. It seeks to limit the voice of the people, but it always does so in the name of the people.

The sinister but shrewd Huey Long once was asked whether we'd ever have fascism in America. "Yes," he replied, "only we'll call it antifascism." In a sense, that's just what's happening. An elite is coming to power under the banner of antielitism. Thus, every change in the rules was made in the name of reform. "Openness" was the battle cry of those who closed things up. What the New Elite extols is precisely what it seeks to destroy. Our most cherished phrases are inverted with a blatancy beyond Lewis Carroll's capacity to mock or Orwell's to portend.

The antidote to this, of course, is to look at deeds, not words. Change is necessary, but when change is proposed in our basic institutions, the test is what that change will actually do, not what is claimed for it.

One of the most recent perversions of the word "open," for example, is in the ominous new push for "open appointments." This is evidenced when public appointments are to be made by elected officials. Take, for instance, the appointment of judges. Formerly, the appointment of a new federal judge would simply be made by the president after consultation with the senator or senators from the state involved and who were of the president's political party. This practice is now much derided, and is said to be too "political." It is pointed out that judgeships have been bestowed purely as reward for past political service. The new alternative is said to be much more "open." Under it, the senator agrees to be guided by a "panel of citizens." The panel screens the names of all judicial applicants and then selects from them a much smaller list from which the senator must then choose. In this manner, it is claimed, judges can be selected by "the people" in a manner free of "politics."

It sounds so right. But when one looks closely at the practice itself, the issue is much less clear. First, the "political" way of selecting judges was always better than is now claimed. Very few scholars of our judicial system would deny that the caliber of our federal bench has been consistently high. The opportunity for political favoritism was always there, of course, but so was something else that mitigated against its use: accountability. Senators and presidents run for election. Their judicial appointments, if tainted, would be a legitimate campaign issue. Only one party at a time can make a particular appointment, so the other party is quite free to comment on that appointment as it will, or even to block its confirmation—as Edward Kennedy discovered when he tried to nominate the unqualified Francis X. Morrisey for the Massachussetts federal bench. The public accountability of those who do the appointing has kept the level of federal judicial appointments very high. The lawyers in a given state have an obvious stake in the ability of their judges, and an angry bar is scarcely an asset to a senator seeking reelection. Those who were appointed in the old way may have been politically active, but they were generally the most qualified of those in the political arena.

And what, really, does "political" mean? Surely there is something to be said for the appointees of a particular administration sharing its values. The politicians who did the appointing were elected by the people because they stood for certain values. Is it so counter to democratic rule for appointees to reflect the same values that the people themselves have chosen? It can indeed be argued that with judges this should not be the case, but that argument cannot be made by those whose code words are "open to the people." The political process can be the best way of assuring that appointments *are* open to the people—in a majoritarian society.

The "citizen panels" that are now being set up to make judicial appointments are seldom composed of ordinary citizens. They are usually referred to as "blue ribbon," which means that they are filled with prominent citizens, well-educated and often of high professional attainment (though not necessarily in the law). An effort is made to make them seem nonpartisan, so their allegiance is likely to be less to any mandate of the voters than to their own social class. It is probable that they are well-intentioned, but this intent could lead merely to the selection of those with similar backgrounds. What guarantee, other than by nomenclature, is there that the "public" interest will be served? Using this test alone, is the new system really superior to the old?

Citizen panels are set up to be "balanced." If there is a woman member, she is said to represent "women." A sixty-eight-year-old man can be claimed as a representative of "senior citizens," and so on. When the panel is fully comprised, each member can be pointed to as standing for some specific constituency. All these different constituencies, when added up, are said to represent "the people." But of course they do not. There is a general public good beyond the ken of those who think that enough single-issue parts can make a whole. If the panel members take their labels seriously, the woman member is looking for women to appoint to the bench, the senior citizen is vigilant about disqualification because of age, and the businessman or labor leader will be looking for those who share their points of view. If they take their labels *very* seriously, then no one will be interested primarily in finding good judges. No one's first concern will be the general quality of justice. That would be the people's first concern, of course, but despite all the labels, the people are not being consulted. The citizen panel is truly the enemy of the people because its members identify either with the upper-middle class from which most of them were chosen, or with the specific constituencies each is said to represent and whose narrow concerns are often irrelevant to the general task at hand.

The use of such citizen panels has spread. In some states, many of the appointments formerly made by an elected governor have now been handed over to the new committees. This arrangement can buy some temporary peace for the beleaguered governor. He can assign to the appointing panel the leaders of all the new factions that have been making his public life difficult—and then they can appoint all their friends. A committee, unlike one lone official, does not run for reelection, and it avoids accountability merely through its corporate state. These panels, elected by no public vote, are now entrusted with myriad state appointments. If a governor appointed a crony to, say, the state board of education, there would likely to be an outcry. When the citizen panel appoints its cronies, there's much less accountability—and much less chance that the appointee represents values sanctioned by the voters. The power to appoint is a lofty one. There has been a great and growing shift in that power away from the mandate of the ballot box. And this is happening in the name of giving the public more control.

So much that has happened in recent years has achieved the same result. One might almost posit that the greater the use of the word "reform," the more likely that the public will be deprived of participation.

This is even apparent in the realm of campaign financing. A plethora of new laws has changed the role of the contributor. As always, these laws were enacted in the name of rectifying what was in fact a real abuse. There were, indeed, "fat cats" whose huge campaign gifts gave them special favor(s) at court. It was desirable that this be changed, but perhaps the solution is now worse than the problem. In federal campaigns, for example, the maximum individual contribution now permitted by law is one thousand dollars. The obvious intent of this "reform" was to limit the influence that really big contributors could buy. It is doubtful that this goal was accomplished. New arrangements, such as corporation Political Action Committees (PACs), ensure that large interests can still finance their way to influence.

But what of the individual contributors? The thousand-dollar rule has greatly changed the type of contributors, but not necessarily in the way that lawmakers intended. It is true that the role of the really big individual contributor has been limited. Gifts of fifty or one hundred thousand dollars are a thing of the past. When a candidate for federal office sets out now to raise money he or she must look to a new group of contributors. Once it was enough to ask five or ten very rich supporters to help get things going; now the appeal must be widened. The really small contributor will not be solicited, however; five and ten and twenty-five dollar checks are still too difficult and expensive to raise within the time constraints of a campaign. Instead, the candidate looks at the thousand dollar market. Instead of five or ten bankrollers, he or she will now seek out five hundred or a thousand—those who can give anywhere from one hundred dollars up to a thousand.

These new contributors must be well off, though not necessarily very rich. Upper-middle-class professional types comprise the target group. Individually, very few of them could finance a whole campaign; togther they are the new ball game.

The federal campaign restrictions were not deliberately passed to strengthen the hand of the New Elite, but they have had that effect. The phone calls to five friends have been supplanted by the cocktail party for a hundred like-minded members of a new and affluent class. Contributions still buy influence—but the purchasers have changed.

Those contributions were never more desperately needed by the office-seeker. Political parties used to be of very great assistance in getting their candidates elected. They furnished money and workers and the sanction of a label that for many voters was enough to attract their support. Merely obtaining party endorsement used to be so helpful that many candidates didn't have to spend all their time raising money—or be rich themselves. Once, the strong political party permitted those without great wealth or a famous name to run successfully for office. As the role of the party diminished, however, media campaigning filled the gap. It is a very expensive filler. Now the candidate without private means or public fame can survive only by raising huge amounts of money. Precluded from relying on the rich and unable to bother with the poor, a candidate's sources are very limited. The maximum allowable gift is so low in terms of the total needed that there isn't enough time to solicit each contributor individually. The candidate must find them in a group.

There are groups which are prepared to fill the need, people who can be gathered together on behalf of the outlook they share. They are prepared to bring their checkbooks and kick in several hundred dollars apiece for the candidates with whom they can identify. One is not speaking here of special-interest giving, of the chiropractors or stockbrokers who have specific bills they want passed, but of the general contributor who can afford to participate in a meaningful way. Because of the changes in campaign finance laws, the role of the rich has been reduced in this arena while the role of the well-off professionals has been very much enhanced.

There is nothing wrong with people giving money to candidates they like. In fact, it's supposed to be part of the system. The problem is that not everyone can participate. Independent financing of campaigns is increasingly the prerogative of the upper-middle class. The point isn't that this may be better than restricting that role to the very rich; it doesn't really matter which group is "better." What does matter is that no one group, however well-educated or enlightened, ought to have such a hold on the candidates. It is inevitable that candidates will come to say and do the things that please their meaningful contributors. Those who do not do so will be less likely to raise the funds necessary for survival.

Campaign financing was not really "reformed" by expanding its base from some hundreds of the rich to some thousands of the comfortable. (The contributors didn't necessarily become less conservative, either; a significant number of the former big givers favored liberal causes.) The worst of those who used to give huge amounts were buying access to presidents and senators; their contributions were really investments, meant to swell their egos or their wallets. To say that this was wrong is to embrace the obvious. What is not so obvious, but just as true, is that the new practice is as corruptive of democracy as was the former campaign financing system. The real corruption is not the intent, but the act: the buying of public servants by a privileged few. The essence of corruption is not lost through purity of motive; a bribe to advance a cause is still a bribe, and the public is still shortchanged.

One hears that the financing of elections is now more "open." But in this context above all, what can "open" possibly mean? Open to whom? To those who can afford to donate several hundred dollars? Anatole France said that "the law, in its majestic equality, forbids the rich as well as the poor, from sleeping under bridges." This was a comment on the meaning of equality. The campaign financing laws are a comment on openness—on what openness has lately come to mean. With Anatole France, the irony was intentional.

So much of what is being bought and sold under the label of greater public participation is really just the shift of power to the New Elite. The members of that elite may not in fact be either devious or hypocritical. They probably do believe that access to power is now open because it's more open to *them*. They are their own universe. They mean themselves when they say "everyone" and probably even when they speak of "the people." They aren't so much deliberately exclusionary as self-absorbed. This distinction scarcely mitigates what they do.

What they do is often well intended. It isn't all a matter of deliberate power grabs. In fact, some of the events set in motion by the New Elite eventually work against its interests. An example of such unforeseen consequences is the campaign disclosure law, an innovation which requires that all political contributions to federal candidates be made public. The goal of this law was surely laudable. Ethical conflicts of interest would be revealed to the public gaze. To some extent, this goal has been realized. But it had other, less positive effects. To many honest citizens, the requirement of public disclosure operated as a threat. Lawyers, businessmen, all those who might transact business with the federal government were afraid to offend incumbents by contributing to their rivals. This was particularly true when the incumbent seemed likely to be reelected. It can be very uncomfortable to have one's congressman as an active foe. It therefore became more difficult for challengers to wage a serious campaign; too many of their supporters were afraid to give. As a result, public campaign disclosure has been something of a bonanza for incumbents. Those who are already in office have been given a stronger lease. It's hard to see the benefit to the New Elite in this, aside from the general advantage it gains whenever free elections are thwarted.

Much of the damage inflicted by the New Elite is not part of some sinister plot. High civic motive is often involved. The danger stems not so much from any crafty goal as from the strong proclivity to tinker with our basic institutions. Perhaps the greatest mischief of the New Elite is in the rapacity with which it seeks to rewrite our basic rules. Change is often a necessity, but it's not always a mandate. The really dangerous notion now abroad in the land is that *everything* should be changed right away—and changed not through convincing the populace of a better course of action but by fiat, through a changing of the rules.

The cause of all this agitation is always a specific event. In every society, things go wrong. When they do, it's only natural to try to prevent their recurrence. This is the point at which the New Elite has been most dangerous. Its members are so used to adjusting mistakes on paper that they think they can do the same with everything that disappoints them in life. In public life, this insistence on altering structure also reflects disdain for the majority. Other citizens see things they don't like, but their first response isn't to change the rules. If their candidate loses an election, their reaction isn't to restructure the way elections are held. They retain the hope that someday their candidate will win. In the practice of majority rule, everyone loses sometimes. Most people are sustained through disappointment, though, by the possibility of being part of a future majority. If your cause is right, others will join it and someday you will prevail.

The New Elite has no such hope predicated on faith in the majority for the New Elite has no such faith. It does not think the majority is wise enough to come to share the views that one small class already holds. And even if the majority is finally persuaded, why should progress be deferred until this comes to pass? Majority sanction isn't seen as that which makes this progress right, only as that which makes it happen. Things can also happen through changing the rules; to the members of the New Elite, that's good enough.

They have been very busy. In the political arena, almost everything now happens under rules that have recently been changed. The worse things get, the worse they will get, as every failure in the innovations is used to justify yet more change. We're coming to the point where no election will be governed by the same rules as the one which preceded it. We're nearly to the point where complexity and confusion and rapidly shifting guidelines have shaken most citizens from the hope of participation. Politics is dying, gravely ill from too many transfusions.

What is needed is not an end to change. That would be as fatal as its surfeit. What is called for is skepticism. We would do well to recall Burke's adage that not all change is reform. We must learn to distinguish between the rhetoric of reform and the real thing. The habit of compliance with that rhetoric must cease. The test cannot be only whether there is a problem to be solved; the solution must stand on its own merits, too. People must ask not only "Is something broken?" but also "How will this fix it?" We should apply careful consideration before we permit anything to be done in our name.

The subject of rules, boring to most voters, has been the prerogative of only a few. That must change, else everything will be the prerogative of the New Elite. People must be made aware of what is going on—and they can be. The rules of politics are no more complex than those of baseball. The media could be of help here—if television and newspapers would devote one-tenth of the coverage to political rules that they do to the candidates' daily gaffes. The media must do more than simply share this information with the public; it must strive as well to adopt the same skepticism toward reform proposals that it has maintained so vigilantly toward campaign promises. All of these rules changes *are* campaign promises—and not one of them has been kept. With many of the most promising students in the country stampeding into investigative journalism, it is hoped that some of them will take a crack at the biggest story of the decade.

The greatest change in the way we govern ourselves as a people has taken place quietly, out of sight. If the shroud is lifted, the people—as always—will know what to do.

CHAPTER 4

AN END TO ISSUES

Why did John Anderson, a relatively conservative Republican, attract so many of the nation's most liberal voters away from the Carter-Mondale camp?

What accounts for the dramatic growth of single-issue politics?

In 1976, how did an unknown, former one-term governor of Georgia ever get to be the presidential nominee of the nation's largest party? And why did he nearly lose the campaign that he began with so massive a lead?

Why did so many primary voters in 1980 reject George Bush and turn to Ronald Reagan, when their stands on the issues are almost identical?

How can the New Right be making so much progress in America at precisely the same time that most citizens are becoming more liberal in terms of specific issues?

Why are the choices so poor, the campaigns so long, the results so puzzling?

Each of these questions has the same answer. They are all part of the same story.

The change in the rules and structure of democracy is only half that story. The other half is just as ominous, but much more visible—so visible, in fact, that it's been taken completely for granted and therefore, in a curious way, has hardly been noticed at all.

This half of the story concerns the change in attitude. It matters far more than changing the rules, for it involves a change in the way we see things. The New Elite has succeeded in altering the way most Americans look at politics. Now there is a different standard governing who we vote for and why we vote for them. The political climate has been utterly transformed.

What has transpired is that the New Elite's basic approach to politics has been adopted by almost everyone else. Not its goals nor its candidates, to be sure, but its attitude toward the political process.

There is some irony that this approach is now being employed by the Left Behinds to thwart the New Elite's drive to power. Blinded by the same narrow vision, each side wages war against the other. The casualty of the conflict is democracy itself, and no one really wins. The choices get worse and worse and have less meaning.

All the visible problems stem from this new approach: the growth of single-issue politics, the inanity of recent campaigns, the absence of ideas, the incompetence of candidates, and voters who vacillate between apathy and anger.

What is the New Elite's political attitude, that unique vision that has spread with such disastrous results? At its core lies the simple notion that issues no longer count. In America today there is a widespread preoccupation with image rather than issues, especially among the best-educated citizens, and this can be traced directly to the New Elite; after all, it is the cornerstone of their approach to politics.

To the New Elite, it makes perfect sense. An emphasis on issues is the concern of those who wish to promote a particular philosophy. The New Elite has no philosophy, no ideology it seeks to impose on others, and no agenda of laws to be passed.

Its members sometimes agree that a particular measure should be enacted or defeated, but such specific goals are not their true quarry; what they really want is to rule by themselves.

All their lives they have been told that they were superior to the rest of the populace—superior in intellectual ability as measured by certain tests. For them, that is enough. The most important tasks are awarded to those with the highest scores. This is essentially their view of government and it helps explain why the New Elite has so few precise views on the issues. For a group whose favorite political claim is to being completely "issue oriented," it is astonishingly devoid of any platform or agenda directed toward solving specific problems. When asked to produce one, its members invariably cite the problems, not the answers. A New Elitist "explains" his program by saying he is concerned with the economy and health care and the environment and so on. He is simply identifying the problems.

This is understandable. If one subscribes to the notion that one's group is best qualified to solve society's problems, perhaps all that *is* required is their identification. Precise answers are unnecessary because no other group could produce better ones! More to the point, precise answers are undesirable because they are subject to rational analysis, criticism, or attack. Legitimate fault may be found, even by some who are obviously not as well qualified to govern. If the Left Behinds are permitted to challenge a policy of the New Elite—particularly if the challenge is well-reasoned or successful—they undermine the New Elite's principle that only the New Elite is fit to govern. The New Elite insists that it knows best, and that its policies should be immune from disagreement by the majority. One way to achieve this immunity is never to state the policies at all.

This is analogous to the immunity from criticism that was enjoyed by feudal lords before the age of majority rule. The principle is precisely the same. The feudal lords did not feel that their vassals were incapable of suggestions that would lead to the improvement of things; sometimes they even listened to suggestions from them. The point was that the vassals had no *right* to proffer their views, for the right of governance belonged to one class only. The right to impose a specific view upon the ruling class was unthinkable, even if the view was sound. Clearly, any advantages gained by an improved public policy would be more than offset by its undermining the basic buttress of sovereignty, whether based on divine right or property or any other nonmajoritarian source. It is this immunity to the right of a majority voice to which we are returning; the refusal even to present people with specific programs on which to comment is both evidence and tactic of the New Elite approach.

The New Elite just *assumes* that it should govern. It doesn't realize that the basic question of who should govern ought not to be answered by comparing IQ scores, that measurable intelligence is not the only qualification for making political judgments.

It is something members of the New Elite ought to think about. Even *their* world affords some clues. An individual with the highest score on the standardized Law School Admissions Test has a high probability of receiving good grades in law school. But he has a much less certain probability of being a successful lawyer. Is it because of "personality" factors—character, diligence, charm? Or is success at the bar based in part on some aspects of intelligence not yet measurable by the standard tests? Or is "personality" itself an aspect of intelligence? Is "judgment"? The critical point about these questions is that they have not been answered. We know only that certain specific skills can be tested with rough accuracy; we do not know what significance should be accorded to possession of those skills. We measure only those facets of intelligence that we know how to measure. We do not know what portion of "intelligence" those facets comprise. And we do not know what role in human performance measured "intelligence" by itself provides.

But the New Elite thinks it knows. In terms of its own role in the scheme of things, it is blissfully free from doubt. It is confident that its role has been certified by test scores. And it knows what it wants to do.

It wants to elect to office those who are members of the New Elite. It wants to empower its own. It has only one test in the selection and support of candidates: Is he or she a member of the New Elite?

It has been demonstrated that there is no test for admission to the New Elite; members are self-selected. If they think they belong, they do.

The real test of a New Elitist is not intelligence, but the degree of identification with others in the New Elite. Allegiance is to this class and to the justification for its existence and rewards: the certainty that "ability" can be measured and one's role in society accordingly assigned. It would undermine their new-found status to acknowledge that status might be justified by anything other than measurable skills. The worst threat to their position is the power of values derived from tradition or experience. Those values are the enemy. Their political goal is the rejection of those whose loyalties are to such values.

All voters look for candidates who share their own values. Businessmen like to see a businessman in office—even those whose success in the business world was less than spectacular. Those with strong religious values look with favor on candidates who attend church regularly—even if they may be less than perfectly devout.

The New Elite is no different. It looks for those who believe in the new class. The New Elite is very jealous of competing loyalties, so it looks, with particular fear and vigilance, for those who are loyal to other values—that these candidates may be kept from public office. The New Elite is not searching for good businessmen or good Lutherans or good Southerners or even good people, for that matter. Gifts of character or judgment or diligence are not their first concern. They are seeking their own: candidates loyal to their values only.

The search for such purity is difficult. It is not enough to know a candidate's academic background and previous accomplishments in public or private life. These things can help establish intellectual credentials, but they constitute only a threshold.

What must also be determined is the extent to which the candidate's values are independent of tradition.

It is not easy to identify a candidate in these regards by his or her record on the issues. What a candidate believes is not as important as how he or she came to believe it. They might have traveled to that place down the alien path of tradition or reached those conclusions by virtue of upbringing, religious faith, class hatred, or personal consideration. If so, they cannot be truly embraced by the New Elite, even though it shares their conclusions on the issues. It matters not merely what the candidate does but *why*. The New Elite reserves special scorn for those who "do the right thing for the wrong reason."

It is exceedingly important to the New Elite that the candidate reject the role of tradition. What a candidate says is not nearly as much of a clue as *how* it is said. What matters is appearance, nuance, style. Details about personal life are terribly important. A midwestern Presbyterian who becomes a devotee of Zen will appeal to the New Elite because he is displaying independence of the values in which he was raised. Certain words and phrases, clothes, and values are applauded by the New Elite; the candidates who distinguish themselves by these will be announcing their identity to a very receptive audience.

In politics, the New Elite focuses exclusively on style. Issues matter only when they have symbolic value, such as one's readiness to break with tradition. This is particularly true with life-style issues like gay rights and abortion. Attempts to alter tradition through law polarize the public; much stronger emotions are directed toward a local referendum on say, gay rights, than toward issues that have far more impact on most voters.

For the New Elite, such life-style issues are fundamentally important. The real concern is not merely the specific cause they advocate but whether the majority has the right to block a new proposal with no other argument than the force of tradition. With most economic issues, this is not the case. Arguments for or against a tax cut are based on a reasoned analysis of available data. That analysis may be faulty, even half-baked, but at least it pretends to be based on reason. With social issues, though, emotion plays a much larger role. Neither side can really "prove" its case, though each side *feels* that it is right, but finds it very difficult to convert others through the use of reasoned argument. Graphs and charts and logic are to no avail. What matters is how a majority of people feel. When the majority view rests mostly on tradition, the New Elite is particularly infuriated for they are left without an argument to rebut and without figures to challenge. The majority view prevails simply because it is the majority view. Those issues which provoke a sharp response based only on tradition have the greatest symbolic value to the New Elite. They serve as a political litmus test, dividing Us from Them.

This is not to suggest that advocacy of life-style issues is the prerogative of the New Elite. The issues which have split the nation so emotionally in recent years were raised by individuals of many different backgrounds who believed with deep conviction in their causes and they very well may not have been members of the New Elite. Once their issues were publicly raised, however, those issues were the potential jousting ground between the New Elite and the Left Behinds, between those who say "why not?" and those who answer, "tradition."

There is nothing new about people supporting candidates with whom they can identify. It was standard practice half a century ago for tickets to be "balanced" with representatives of the major voting blocs—Italians, Irish, Jews—so that each voter could find at least one candidate whose background he or she might identify with. But everyone on the ticket was part of the same organized political party and subscribed to its platform. They shared a common ideology which was addressed to the majority. That's not true today. The candidate's identity isn't merely a prerequisite nor is class recognition the threshold test of the New Elite. They are the sole preoccupation.

That the New Elite concentrates on life-style issues to the exclusion of all else is exemplified by the candidacy of John Anderson. Anderson had served for twenty years in Congress before campaigning for the presidency. He participated in thousands of roll-call votes, and on a great many of those votes took the conservative side. His voting record—the clearest test of one's stands on the issues—was very much that of a moderate-to-conservative Republican. Yet from the very start his candidacy attracted many liberal voters. Thousands of those who flocked to Anderson, who signed his petitions and sent him money, disagreed with him on nearly every issue. *But they did approve of his well-known stand on abortion.* It was a cornerstone of his campaign. He mentioned it in every speech, and the position became identified with his candidacy.

John Anderson's position on abortion was similar to Jimmy Carter's. Both opposed a constitutional amendment forbidding abortions. The only apparent distinction was that Anderson favored federal funding for abortions and Carter did not. This distinction may have accounted for some of Anderson's appeal to liberal voters, but a great deal of that appeal would seem to have stemmed from the emphasis he gave those views. He talked about this issue so much that it seemed to be his first priority; thus he attracted those who saw it as the most important issue of the campaign.

For those who use only issues as a litmus test, one issue is enough—if the litmus test is good enough. If all one wants is to determine whether a candidate is independent of the forces of tradition, a single issue will suffice. If an issue fixes precisely the candidate's class identity, then reliance on other issues will only dilute the real test.

The New Elite invented single-issue politics, at least the brand that is prevalent today. There have always been single-issue fanatics, of course, but the phenomenon of recent years is unique in several ways. In the past, there were those who started with a cause which eventually became an obsession. Now, it's the other way around: A group begins with a sense of moral imperative which transcends the need for majority support—and finds issues to feed that sense and define its own allies. The single issues that generate such fervor don't really mean that much—even to their supporters; they're primarily symbols, emblems of identity in the new class warfare. In fact, single-issue politics has little to do with politics and even less to do with issues. It's really single-*image* politics, a game in which the point is to identify the players through the image they convey. The identification sought is not one of ideas but of values. Image is the key to finding out just who is who.

This helps explain why single-issue politicians constantly refer to their own moral certainty. The insistence on special moral insight is an acceptable method of disregarding the majority's verdict. The moral reference was not nearly so flagrant in the single-issue movements of the past. At the turn of the century, those whose single issue was the free coinage of silver were fanatic about their cause, but they didn't rest their case on their own moral perceptions. They relied primarily on economic arguments because they hoped to win the majority over to their side. Confident that this was possible, they made their case with this in mind. Theirs was an effort to persuade.

The New Elite does not wish to persuade. It has no faith that the majority can be won over. It doesn't even really *want* to win over the majority because the necessity for doing so implies that the majority knows best and the New Elite believes that *it* knows best. However, to express this view so bluntly would not be prudent, so its members have found a socially acceptable code word: moral. They say "we are morally right" when they mean "we know best." It is impossible to disprove an appeal to moral authority; therefore the necessity to argue one's case in the marketplace of ideas is crisply circumvented. *Reliance on self-proclaimed morality is the necessary corollary to a single-issue politics of which the real point is domination by a special class.*

Another corollary of this approach is the refusal to compromise. This is as old an aspect of politics as stubbornness itself. Lately it's been promoted from a trait to a principle. If one group has total confidence in its own superiority, then it regards compromise as absurd. This is an adjunct to the moral argument and a further rejection of the principle of majority rule, of which compromise is an essential part. The whole idea of majority rule is that many people want many things and that by accommodating those wants through compromise an acceptable decision is attainable. Compromise provides a way of giving credence to several points of view. And that is why it is such anathema to those with one strong point of view, rigid in their beliefs and confident of their superiority. So, "compromise" has become the New Elite's favorite epithet. So pervasive is the New Elite in the realm of opinion-making, so articulate in the propagation of its own fine sense of disdain, that its angry scorn of compromise has been widely adopted. Most citizens have heard so often that a politician is weak because he "compromises" that they regard the use of compromise as a major character flaw.

The recent changes in political rules spawned single-issue politics, and contributed to its growth, but the change in attitude made it a certainty. The new structure drew those whose interest was best served through reliance on image, disregard for a broad range of issues, an aggressive sense of moral superiority as its own sanction, and the effective abolition of compromise as an acceptable political tool. The new structure and the new attitude together have produced a new politics—flagrantly and proudly single-issue in its focus and absolutely fatal to the political system as we knew it.

Although these attitudes were the handiwork of the New Elite, they did not remain its exclusive property for long. Unconsciously at first, and then as a technique for survival, they were gradually adopted by the Left Behinds. Now much of America is engaged in single-issue, image-oriented politics. The strategy of a few has enveloped us all.

The Left Behinds are not stupid at all, and early in the game they sensed that something was very wrong. Without perhaps defining it as such, they perceived instinctively the decay or capture of those majoritarian institutions that traditionally ensured their own response. They realized that political parties, the government itself, and the courts were becoming estranged from them. They heard voices on the national scene that claimed to speak for the people, but they did not recognize those voices; the message they heard was seldom the message that they would have given.

In desperation, the Left Behinds increasingly reserved their trust for those most like themselves. They began to back those of whom they were certain, whose roots and background and values were indisputably the same as their own. So they, too, edged into a preoccupation with image, the least suspect signal they knew of the policies likely to be passed. Image became an obsession for virtually everyone, and for most of the electorate specific statements on the issues became relevant only in relation to their effect on the image of the candidate who uttered them.

Just as this preoccupation with image led the New Elite into single-issue politics, so was the same path followed by the Left Behinds. If the only way to participate in our society was through such single-issue politics, so be it. If the whole point of politics was to distinguish one's friends from one's enemies, so be it. If the search was for the single issue which best symbolized one's allegiance, so be it. If moral rigidity was in and the spirit of compromise out, so be it. These new lessons were soon mastered.

Those lessons were applied with a vengeance—quite literally. In furious response to the perceived attack on its own values, Left Behinds struck back. Some of them did, anyway. Those who still cherished the traditional virtues of civility and accomodation stood back from the fray. Those who still believed that there were many issues to face were unable to narrow their concern. Those without a particular passion other than the longing for good governance were unable to grasp the new techniques. All of these people dropped out. They were forced to abandon the habit of political participation.

But there were others to whom the new climate was positively salubrious. The Left Behinds have their fanatics, too. There have always been those who wished to impose their religious or social views on everyone else and the new way of doing things suited them exactly. It was tailor-made for their zeal.

Once, most single-issue movements were identified with the political left. Now it's the New Right that is having its day—

or perhaps much longer. The forces now expanding their power are those of religious fundamentalism and political reaction. While they've always been around, they were formerly confined to the fringes by lack of majority support. That lack no longer stops them for the majority no longer matters. The majority stays at home. The ranks of the New Right single-issue groups are swollen with an offshoot of that majority—those with traditional values and deep frustration who will join any army that marches against their enemy. The forces that are marching now are often narrow and misdirected, but they are very numerous.

It had to happen. When a society is forced into absolute choices between extreme positions, the forces of tradition usually win. When society adopts a politics of class identification, the largest class-clusters will probably prevail. There are more Left Behinds than members of the New Elite. There are more people who feel strongly about protecting traditional values than those who seek to attack those values. When those values were made the single issue, the ascendancy of the New Right was assured. And it is *easier* for the traditionalists to mobilize in the new structure and climate imposed by the New Elite.

Surely this is not what the New Elite had in mind. The New Elite rejects the ties of religious fundamentalism. Many of its members scorn the dictates of rightist politics, yet these are the forces it has greatly strengthened.

The ultimate irony is that the New Elite has helped enthrone its enemies. The single-issue groups of the New Right could never have achieved their recent successes but for the New Elite. The threshold barrier to single-issue domination—from either the Left or the Right—was a strong two-party system. The necessity for either party to win over a majority was a very moderating influence. The need to put together coalitions of disparate parts meant that the most extreme parts would be excluded from the coalition for there had to be a general level of acceptability. Parties put the brake on extremism. But parties were castigated by the New Elite and gravely weakened through the rule changes. Thus the way for single-issue dominance was cleared.

The New Elite began the process of replacing political parties with single-issue factions to advance its own cause. Now those at the opposite end of the political spectrum are doing the same thing, and this is eliciting shock and anger from the New Elite. They are very quick to denounce the growth of single-issue politics, and don't realize that they are responsible for it. They even continue their own efforts at precisely the same sort of politics; but they prefer to describe their actions as "organizing around issues."

That description is patently unacceptable. Single-issue politics is anti-issues politics. To focus exclusively on one cause is to omit all others. Recently, delegates have been selected for the national conventions of both parties without even having to state their views on the economy or foreign policy. And this is called organizing around issues. Single-issue politics is not politics, and it leads to very bad government. It's a threat to democracy, regardless of which faction eventually prevails. There is no politics any longer. What passes for politics now is a sort of game. The new rules skew the results and the players can compete only through the most bizarre behavior. The viewing public is hopelessly confused.

The last two presidential campaigns testify to what has happened. Each was conducted in a landscape and a climate quite unlike the traditional ones. Both illustrate the changes in structure and behavior that have been forced on our political system by the growth of the New Elite.

THE 1976 CAMPAIGN

The rules that governed the fight for the 1976 nomination were quite different from those that prevailed in 1972. Most important, there were many more state primaries. State after state had dropped the convention system and moved quickly to primaries to escape the scythe of reform. By 1976, the party leaders themselves no longer called the shots. The battle for the nomination was fought in the open, in dozens of state primaries.

To this new battlefield came no end of contestants. Victory for the Democrats seemed possible; since the party had no incumbent, there was a plethora of candidates, announced or not: Henry Jackson, Hubert Humphrey, Lloyd Bentsen, Birch Bayh, Terry Sanford, George Wallace, Morris Udall, Fred Harris, Walter Mondale, Milton Shapp, and even a former governor of Georgia, Jimmy Carter. There were so many of them that the crowded field became a national joke. The conventional wisdom was that the popular vote would be hopelessly fractionated and the final decision made by a handful of party pros. There were so many candidates and so many primaries that it was improbable that any one aspirant could accumulate the necessary number of delegates. The new rules limiting fund-raising activities would make it impossible for one candidate to make himself heard over the rest.

That was not the way it worked out. Despite all the problems just mentioned, there was still a process—the primary system. The choice in most states would be made directly by the voters. Not all the voters, usually not even a majority of those eligible within a given state, would turn out, of course. But hundreds of thousands—sometimes millions—would vote, an aggregate of instinct and mood far larger and more broadly based than the mutilated structure it supplanted. Because of rules that had been altered to counter the New Elite offensive, far more people would participate in the 1976 nomination process than in any previous effort in American history to select a presidential candidate.

Jimmy Carter was probably last on the likely list when he started, but in retrospect and in light of the forces at work, his nomination should not have been surprising. In a nation torn between competing perceptions, he was the logical candidate of the Left Behinds.

His fitness for this role was obvious—and was surely obvious to the Left Behinds. It is difficult to imagine a candidate who more clearly embodied those roots and values they appreciated and whose rejection they opposed. If ever a candidate wore his roots on his sleeve and proclaimed them as the source of his perceptions, it was Jimmy Carter. If the goal for millions of confused voters was to find a spokesman whose strength derived from a sense of place, then attraction was inevitable to the exemplar of Plains.

A small town is the strongest bastion against the New Elite. It is difficult to be born and raised in one without really knowing the people of that place—and not just the people of one class or stratum or level of income but all of the inhabitants. A single town is not a perfect microcosm of the human condition, but it is better in that regard than a neighborhood or a campus. If one knows everybody in town, one knows their faults and their strengths. One sees that judgment and decency and sense have not been gradated into the preserve of a few. A small town is an exercise in governance, for people have had to learn to govern their relations with one another. Civility is the dominant virtue. The role of tradition and the lessons of experience are nowhere else so clear. Small towns, of course, have their drawbacks, too; narrowness, conformity, even bigotry, are common. Special privilege exists side by side with quite distinct social classes. But within those towns a person's identity stems less from some measured test of potential than from a joint response. To be from a small town is to derive one's own identity from a relationship to humanity as a whole; it is the antidote to stratified identity. To be from, to be of, a small town is to be less likely than others to disdain the majority of the human race. The small town permits the perception of the worth of mankind as a whole.

The Carters were clearly not just from, but of, Plains, Georgia. It simply is not possible to describe Jimmy Carter without describing the town of Plains. The association of man and place was unavoidable and, to millions of voters, had enormous symbolic appeal. All the root sources that nurture identity and permit human experience were there. The attraction was not limited to those from the rural South. People in Iowa, too, felt they could perceive the values of a man who taught Sunday school in the church that his father had attended, and his father before him.

So from the start the Carter candidacy was greatly helped by the appearance and perception of his background.

But that was not the only source of his appeal to the Left Behinds. At least as important as who he was was the public's discovery of who he was not. He was not from Washington. This negative virtue proved to be the greatest single source of his support. Virtually every other candidate in the crowded primary field was a longtime member of the Congress. Humphrey, Jackson, Mondale, Bentsen, and Bayh were United States senators. Fred Harris was a former senator. Morris Udall had served in the House of Representatives for more than fifteen years. Terry Sanford, like Carter, was a former governor, but was characterized by his newer roles of college president and chairman of the Democratic Party Charter Commission that had helped to set the new rules. Milton Shapp was the governor of Pennsylvania, but his campaign was slight and late. There was one other governor in the field, George Wallace, and his success at "sending a message" to the Washington establishment was so remarkable that many Democrats at the outset feared he could win their nomination. (Much of Wallace's support was derived from his image as anti-elitist rather than in response to the issues he raised. This explains the remarkable fact that during the 1968 presidential campaign the polls showed Wallace and Eugene McCarthy appealing to many of the same people, evidence of what the growth of the New Elite has done to the role that issues play in the current political process.)

With the exception of Wallace, all the "serious candidates" were creatures of the Congress. In terms of winning primaries, there was nothing worse that they could be.

Washington, D.C., is the perfect symbolic capital of the New Elite. No one there has any roots in the place. Everyone has come from someplace else, and few plan to stay for long. It is a one-industry town, that industry being government, and most of its key personnel got their jobs on the basis of their measurable and measured ability. The résumé and the civil service exam are the passports to admission. Despite all the publicity given political cronyism, nepotism and privilege play less of a role in the vast federal bureaucracy than they do in private industry. Bright young men and women from all over the nation seek admittance on the basis of their college transcripts. What they have in common when they get there is high measured intelligence and no ties of geography or background to bind them. What they do not have, and can never get so long as they stay in Washington, is a sense of the mood or the strengths or even the existence of all those human beings who comprise the rest of the country.

The insularity of these public servants is a very open secret. The national opinion polls show without exception that the public's view of Washington fluctuates only between hatred and dismay. Elected officials, though their jobs are accorded by popular vote, are certainly not exempt from the scorn. They spend all their time in Washington, and so are sensed to be allies of the New Elite. The public is not eager to promote one of them to the presidency. The virulence with which senators and representatives are regarded is partially explained by the fact that, until they got into the primaries, none of them seemed to be aware that they were even disliked.

In terms of what the Left Behinds wanted and what they opposed, Jimmy Carter struck many as the candidate to support. It was Plains versus Washington. Carter won enough primaries to ensure a first-ballot nomination, something that had not been thought possible for any of the aspirants in the presidential quest. Apart from the Wallace threat, his only serious primary competition came tellingly enough from another governor, Jerry Brown of California, who was even more outspoken than Carter in his revilement of Washington types.

When Carter actually picked up the nomination in July in New York, his popularity was astonishingly high. It was not only delegates who were scrambling to come on board. The general public, too, had responded to his campaign. The polls showed Carter leading his likely opponent, the incumbent president of the United States, by a margin of more than 30 percent. Seldom has a candidate left a convention with more visible evidence of popular support. The prospect had no precedent. Hard-headed analysts looked at the polls and concluded that Carter might actually carry every one of the fifty states.

Yet he nearly lost. Carter's sudden and accelerating plunge in the polls began just after the convention and continued unabated through an election so close that for twelve hours after the polls closed no one could be certain who had won.

Carter's decline after the nomination resulted from precisely the same polarized perceptions that had accounted for his popularity before it. The disparate views of the New Elite and the Left Behinds continued to define the nature of the contest, and image remained the trigger of perception. The problem was that Carter was perceived differently after his nomination than before it. *He* did not change, but people's perception of him did. This can be attributed to the nature of his postconvention campaign.

One of the first things that candidate Carter did was meet with five Catholic bishops to discuss the issue of abortion. Carter's views on the subject, which were consistent with the Democratic party platform, were not acceptable to the bishops, and they said so publicly. The network news programs showed them rejecting Carter's stand. In that context, it looked as if they were rejecting Carter, too. One bishop actually speculated on the air as to whether voting for Jimmy Carter might not be a mortal sin.

Shortly thereafter, Carter journeyed to the state of Washington to address the national convention of the American Legion. He repeated to the Legionnaires his oft-stated intention to pardon draft resisters and was resoundingly booed.

A short time later, he had a well-publicized meeting with Ralph Nader, at the conclusion of which Carter promised that when elected he would "out-Nader Nader."

These events and others like them, taken as a whole, contributed to a new perception of candidate Carter. Confusion and anxiety began to plague the Left Behinds.

The exact cause of this distress had very little to do with the issues Carter was espousing. Indeed, if the polls are accurate, each of the positions Carter took was supported at the time by a majority of the population. If a climate existed in which issues were viewed on their merits, Carter's pronouncements would have caused him little trouble. But that was not the case. The Left Behinds were forced into the same framework as their rivals. (Image permeates issues; the search is for personnel, not policies.) What the Left Behinds saw was not a majoritarian stand on abortion but a candidate rebuffed by the elders of a church. They saw a candidate jeered at a convention whose delegates looked and sounded much like they did themselves. However popular the cause of protecting consumer rights, the vow to "out-Nader Nader" suggested a zeal for social experiment that bordered on excess.

And then came the *Playboy* interview. In light of the nature of current campaigns and this campaign in particular, one can scarcely imagine a more disastrous event for the candidate. It was precisely because no real issue was involved that the episode had such a calamitous effect. That Carter's remarks, in context, were not only reasonable but moral is quite beside the point. The fact of the interview caused the damage, not its content. The perception of a man who discussed sexual matters in a magazine viewed as an almost perfect symbol of moral offensiveness by those who hold with a traditional style of life and comment was at great variance with the earlier image of Carter. At best, it made him look inconsistent. At worst, it made him appear the ally, not the antithesis, of the new class whose tastes and boldness are unrestrained by traditional patterns of conduct. It is incredible that an incident of this sort should have so dominated the process of choosing a president, but its force and impact simply cannot be denied.

It would be wrong to suggest that Carter's postnomination campaign consisted wholly of image disasters. Some things went very well. Most useful in gaining the final result was all the time that the candidate spent at home. For a month following the Democratic convention, Carter very wisely stayed in Plains. Every night the network news showed him walking in his fields, greeting his neighbors, cleaning out his mother's pond; the image of a man who was part of a place intensified. This image was very helpful to many voters, though not all. People in the South and in small towns everywhere were reassured by what they saw. However, there were those in the large cities who shared Carter's values but could not perceive them in an environment so alien to their experience. (Image is much less inherently helpful in winning a majority than in mollifying the demands of a single-interest group.) Carter probably received the votes of most of those people who had ever drained a pond. The background he provided from Plains immunized him just enough from all the other media gaffes to eke out the final victory. (It should be noted that Carter's election was not really so close in the popular vote as in the electoral college. Despite all the problems, he did receive an absolute majority of all the votes cast; that is more than John Kennedy did in 1960, or Richard Nixon in 1968. Carter was the first nonincumbent to be elected by a majority of the votes cast since Dwight Eisenhower in 1952.)

The campaign of 1976 marked the counterattack of the Left Behinds. The establishment of many new state primaries permitted Carter to win the nomination. He triumphed in these more majoritarian forums because he suggested values that are shunned by the New Elite. This accounted for his final victory, too, though its effect was much diminished when he appeared to be representing other values. Some have said that his mistake was in becoming too "liberal" after the nomination. This view is incorrect. It is not only a mistake to view the campaign in terms of liberal versus conservative ideology, it is a mistake to view it in terms of ideology at all. The controlling force was image. If issues alone had been what mattered, Carter's postnomination conduct would have won him more, not less, support. The country is not becoming more conservative, it is becoming more liberal— in terms of specific issues. The "hot" liberal issues—national health care, gun control, legalized abortion—enjoy the support of a majority of the public, and the polls indicate that that support is steadily growing. *The shift to the right that so many commentators perceive is really the revolt of the Left Behinds.* Issues figure prominently in this revolt only when they signal the presence of the enemy. Advocacy of a position that enjoys majority support can actually cost a candidate that support if people see the issue involved not on its merits but as a device of those who seek to restrict the right of majority rule. This is why the number of people who identify themselves to pollsters as "liberal" is declining, even as public support for liberal positions grows.

The advocacy of liberal views is not an electoral danger so long as the advocate preserves his true identity as defender of the majority's ultimate right to govern. This is not always an easy task, as Mr. Carter learned. The advancement of the liberal agenda has been seriously stalled by the growth and threat of the New Elite. Public wariness has transformed the political arena into the least receptive forum for dispassionate appraisal of the issues. The net result: the New Elite has tainted the very policies it reasonably hopes to promote. So it is those who hold with the liberal agenda who should be first to defend our majoritarian institutions against the growing threat.

THE 1980 ELECTION

The first point to note about the 1980 campaign is its length. It lasted for several years. There were Republican hopefuls out on the hustings as early as 1978. Few were surprised by this; people are becoming accustomed to campaigns of great duration.

This is yet another depressing legacy from the New Elite. When political parties played a strong role in selecting their own candidates, they were able to do so with dispatch. But candidate selection is now performed by the primaries—lots of them. The new procedures take much more time, which may not be entirely bad; if the voters are forced to survey the field without any help from a screening committee, they need plenty of time to give the least stable contenders a chance to reveal their faults.

Another reason the challengers started so early is that the incumbent looked so vulnerable. The extreme unpopularity of the Carter presidency was well defined by the polls. Carter's rating chart looked like the Grand Teton range; each succeeding valley was lower than the last. At one point he broke the record, achieving a lower rating even than Nixon at the nadir of Watergate.

Carter's performance in office was directly related to the way he got there. The most frequent complaints about him were that he was obsessed with detail, lacked passion, and showed no leadership, but those are precisely the qualities that are rewarded by today's primary system. Those defects gained Carter the nomination. Obsession with detail pays off with a primary public that has little way of judging the candidate's competence; a long recitation of boring facts suggests that the reciter is prepared for the job he seeks. Lack of passion is essential in surviving the primaries; the voters' first concern in today's anarchic system is to weed the lunatics out of the race, and passion might indicate instability. Leadership is a detriment to the primary candidate because real leadership draws opposition, and the prize generally goes to the least offensive.

If these seem like very strange tests for selecting a president, blame the system. If Carter's performance in office was so disappointing to the voters, blame the primary system for that, too. That system *guaranteed* that his performance in the White House would be what it was. The flaws that Carter showed in office were precisely the "skills" that got him there. His presidency was the direct—indeed, the inevitable—result of a decade of uncritical political reform.

Most people didn't see this, didn't really focus on how Carter came to office, but many came to wish that he would not be returned. It seemed increasingly possible that he would be defeated in his reelection bid.

But defeated by whom? There were a number of Republican candidates. Former President Gerald Ford was considered to have the best chance of defeating Carter. He had nearly beaten him in 1976, and Carter's popularity had greatly eroded since then. Reluctant to comply with the new requirement of campaigning through dozens of primaries for the nomination, however, Ford held back. The other candidates—John Anderson, Howard Baker,

George Bush, John Connally, Jack Kemp, and Ronald Reagan—did not. It is significant that three of the major contenders were not currently employed. Bush and Connally and Reagan were free of any obligations but those of the campaign trail. They had learned well one lesson from Carter's victories in 1976: There are now so many primaries to run in that success requires a full-time effort. The nominee must do nothing but campaign for several years. If he holds a job, even one of leadership in the Senate, he might as well stay out of the race.

After many grueling primaries, the choice was down to Reagan and Bush. The significance here is not who won, but why. Philosophically, the two were very close. Both were conservative Republicans. To hear their supporters talk, however, they might have been from separate planets. They attracted entirely different followings. To call the Bush people "liberal" and the Reagan supporters "conservative," as almost everyone did, is to show how meaningless those labels have become. What divided the two candidates was not economics or foreign policy but one or two life-style issues that became the focus of their contest. To both sides, those issues had symbolic value—they were the tip-offs to the class identity of the Ivy League lawyer and the movie star who had been raised in a small town. The search for class identity has always been part of politics, but the extraordinary role of style in the Bush-Reagan runoff was evidence that the new political tests are not applied solely within the Democratic party.

But the Democratic party does provide a more dramatic example of just how powerful those tests have become. The sudden collapse of the Kennedy candidacy attests the recent changes in our politics.

So total was Edward Kennedy's collapse that it is now difficult to recall that he began as the strong front-runner. Every poll and pundit had once agreed on that point. There was a time at the start of the campaign when almost no one really doubted Kennedy's ability to wrest the nomination from Carter, despite Carter's incumbency. The question was always whether Kennedy would, not could, dump Carter. The conventional wisdom was that if Kennedy declared his candidacy, he would attract so much immediate support that Carter would have to drop out of the race.

The conventional wisdom was wrong. It was based on conventional politics, not the climate of today. A funny thing happened to Kennedy on the way to the nomination. He ran into a political system that had been totally transformed.

The evaporation of his support is generally explained by the Chappaquidick episode and by some inept performances at the start of his campaign. These undoubtedly played a role, but Chappaquidick was scarcely a last-minute revelation; it had been in the public consciousness for years and it had not kept Kennedy from his early lead in the polls. Although the interview with Roger Mudd was a disaster, it's difficult to exclusively credit this one incident, or even several like it, with the phenomenal reversal of Kennedy's fortunes.

What really happened to Kennedy was that he tried to practice traditional politics. There is no place for politicians now that politics is dead. The Kennedy campaign illustrates the futility of the traditional approach in today's altered climate.

Kennedy was a very traditional candidate who tried to appeal to the traditional Democratic coalition—blue-collar workers, ethnics, minorities, liberals. To win them over he relied on the glue that had always caused these parts to adhere: an emphasis on economic issues. The time seemed right for this approach: the economy was greatly troubled, unemployment was high, and inflation had robbed many of their savings. The oil companies loomed as exactly the sort of corporate giants against whom the Democratic voters could unite. Kennedy had largely preempted the issues that should have appealed to the old coalition: jobs, gas rationing, national health care. In terms of the way things used to work, his optimism was understandable.

His campaign never got off the ground. It failed because it was based on issues—and issues no longer count. Everyone is affected by the economy and economic arguments were a standard way of winning majority support, yet economic issues have been the most thoroughly disregarded. Institutions and attitudes have been so altered to bypass majority sentiment that the only issues that count today are those which symbolize the social class allegiance of the candidates.

Kennedy went after the majority when the real prize was the single-issue groups. The way to win now is to attract support from enough single-issue groups to make up more than half the delegates. Fifty-one percent of the delegates collected in this fashion do not really constitute a "majority," for they do not agree on any one thing other than temporary support of the same candidate. There is no basis for governance. What Kennedy attempted, in a very old-fashioned way, was to win over a majority on the basis of agreement on at least one issue—the economy. It didn't work because candidates can't win delegates that way anymore.

Kennedy was not above appealing to the single-issue groups himself. He tried to reach the liberal single-issue groups on the basis of his stands on the E.R.A., abortion, and nuclear power. But the support he received from those quarters was lukewarm. To understand this is to understand everything. Most single-issue zealots do not want mere agreements on their issue. An issue is to them a clue, a way of determining the candidate's ability and allegiance. Kennedy's identity smacked too much of the politician, and his allegiance to blue-collar workers and ethnic groups was too well proclaimed.

In John Kennedy's time, one could appeal to both the working class and the New Elite. Edward Kennedy discovered that that is no longer possible because the political framework has changed too drastically. If a candidate's first concern is with a true majority, his views on the issues may be irrelevant. To be a "politician" in the old sense of putting together a traditional coalition is no longer acceptable.

The point is not that without these changes Kennedy would have won—or deserved to. Most likely, he would have lost—if not the nomination, then the general election. He was running as a traditional liberal at a time when many voters from all backgrounds were rejecting liberal policies. But he was rejected as well by some who *agreed* with his policies—or said they did. Perhaps those with professional careers that were comfortable and secure had grown less concerned with the plight of the poor. Surely many who claimed to side with Kennedy on such matters ended up withholding their support. If they actually did agree with him on the issues, they didn't base their votes on it.

Carter and Reagan each arrived at their respective conventions with more than enough votes to be nominated. This doesn't mean that the conventions were not worth observing. Indeed, they broke new ground. Each put into its platform a plank of unprecedented single-issue rigidity. In terms of tactics, both planks were radical departures from what either party had ever dared do before.

The Republican platform of 1980 commits the GOP "to work for the appointment of judges at all levels of the judiciary, who respect traditional values and the sanctity of innocent human life." In other words, no one can be appointed to the bench who would permit the right to abortion in any circumstances. Of course, many Americans share this view of abortion. But no political party has ever before enunciated a single-issue test for appointment to the judiciary. This is a wholly new development in our political (and legal) tradition.

The Democrats were not to be outdone. *Their* platform officially instructs the party apparatus "to withhold financial and technical campaign support from any candidate who does not support the Equal Rights Amendment." As with the Republicans, the shocker here is not the position taken but the unprecedented means of implementing it. A single-issue test has been proclaimed for any candidate requiring Democratic party support. The issue happens to be one that most Democrats (and most Americans) do already endorse. But that is not the point. A single issue has become an absolute test for party support. It will be interesting to see where this precedent will lead.

Under our previous political system, a platform might well have condemned abortion or extolled the E.R.A. What could not have happened is that either issue—any issue—would become the dispositive test of party membership or support.

Neither platform plank could have passed at a majoritarian convention. Many of the delegates at both the 1980 conventions got there as members of single-issue groups. (More than half the Democratic delegates were public employees; they may have felt that this constituted a majority of sorts.) They were answerable only to those single-issue groups; neither Kennedy nor Carter supported the E.R.A. plank, and Reagan did not want the abortion test, but none of the candidates had much control over "their" delegates. Too many of the people at both conventions were not delegates of a candidate or even of a party, but were single-issue delegates. The planks they shouted into being were a logical extension of the politics that got them on the floor—and are the clearest possible expression of what our politics has come to, and where it is going.

Once the conventions had chosen their tickets, the reaction of the public was one of apathy and dismay. There was widespread dissatisfaction with the two parties' choices. The decision of whom to support was frequently made on the negative basis of avoiding someone even worse. The phrase "lesser of two evils" was used so often to describe the Carter-Reagan choice that it became the unofficial slogan of the campaign. People became even less enchanted with politics than they had been. One often heard the complaint that political parties themselves were no good; the quality of the contenders was used to support this thesis. What did not occur to many was that neither party really selected "its" nominee. If the nomination process truly had been in the hands of party professionals, it is doubtful that either Carter or Reagan would have emerged as a nominee. (The Kennedy camp realized this, and waged an unsuccessful rules fight to permit the delegates to vote for the candidate of their choice. The Carter forces succeeded in keeping the delegates bound to the dictates of the primaries. The Carter position was probably right in maintaining that rules—even bad ones—should not be changed in the middle of process, but its insistence that this position would effectuate "the will of the people" was not borne out by the post-convention polls.)

Of course the choice was not only between Carter and Reagan. There was a third candidate as well. The John Anderson candidacy is an almost perfect barometer of the times. It tells us what we've come to.

The Anderson candidacy is as close as we've come yet to a presidential campaign by and for the New Elite. It first qualifies for this distinction by virtue of the fact that Anderson was not the candidate of any party. He had been a lifelong Republican, but he ran as an independent. Political parties are a threat to the New Elite. Even greatly weakened and partly captured by their enemies, parties by their nature suggest a breadth of support and concern that is anathema to the antimajoritarians. To bypass the need for parties completely would hasten the day when majority support could be dispensed with. A candidate without a party permits the politics of faction without restraint.

There had been many third-party candidates for the presidency, but John Anderson's candidacy was something new. He was not a third-party candidate. He was not the candidate of any party. That was the whole point.

George Wallace and Henry Wallace each had gone through the trouble of manufacturing a party structure to give legitimacy to their campaigns. In 1980, Ed Clark and Barry Commoner ran as the standard-bearers of the Libertarian Party and the Citizens Party, respectively. The populist heroes of the past, Debs and LaFollette, were not so populist as to go it alone. They ran as Socialist and Progressive. Even Teddy Roosevelt's abortive attempt to get back in the White House made use of the Progressive Party label (though the public preferred "Bull Moose"). It may never have occurred to some of these men that one could run for president independent of any party structure at all.

It occurred to John Anderson. He understood much better than most commentators (who, curiously, kept referring to him as a "third party" candidate) what his candidacy was all about.

When he needed a running mate, a vice-presidential candidate
to fulfill certain legal requirements, he did not organize a convention or even call a meeting to come up with the requisite
name. He just asked Pat Lucey to run with him, and Lucey said
yes. The fact that Anderson was a Republican and Lucey a Democrat was irrelevant—or, in a sense, highly relevant because it
showed that formal party allegiance was of no concern to this
campaign.

Some of the third parties of the past had been mere fronts—
temporary expediencies to help get a charismatic leader on the
ballot. Even candidates as well-known and forceful as George
Wallace or Teddy Roosevelt had sensed that to gain votes one
needed the appearance of a party.

John Anderson was the first to realize that one could gain
votes through the appearance of *no* party. There had come into
being a new class to whom such disassociation was the highest
qualification for support. There were many educated and affluent
voters who hated the very idea of political parties, and saw the
abandonment of that idea as a decided plus. Those people supported Anderson not despite but *because* he was not the candidate
of any party. He was not part of any large institution that might
require the temporizing links of majoritarian consent.

Others had sought the presidency without a chance to win.
Ed Clark did not think he would be elected president in 1980,
nor did George Wallace in 1968 or LaFollette in 1924. Each
probably thought he was advancing a cause, or at least publicizing
a point of view. Each represented a framework for addressing
the nation's problems, whether that framework was based on
untested utopianism or outright bigotry.

John Anderson was not part of that tradition. He seems to
have run because he thought he could win. There was such widespread disapproval of the other candidates that this may have
seemed plausible. It is difficult to point to any other motive. He
did not appear to be the spokesman for a particular school of
thought. His views on this issue or that may have been admirable,

but they didn't seem to result from a distinct philosophy consistently applied. There was no particular cause of which he stood as the head.

Not all his supporters were members of the New Elite. A number of Americans were so opposed to both Carter and Reagan that they saw in Anderson a safe harbor for protest votes. It seems not to have occurred to them that the major party choices were not accidental, that they were the direct result of recently inflicted party weakness. If the choices were bad because the parties had been abandoned, things were unlikely to improve by abandoning the parties still further. What was needed was transfusion, not more bleeding, of the lifeblood of citizen participation.

The lack of any party qualified Anderson for New Elite support. The lack of any broad program based on shared and recognizable values cinched it. It was often heard from those supporting Anderson that "concern for the issues" had brought them to that allegiance. In fact, he focused on so few issues that this could scarcely have been the case. It is doubtful that many rallied to his banner solely in support of a fifty-cents-a-gallon tax on gasoline. People said they supported Anderson because of "what he stood for," but what he stood for seems largely to have been a matter of who he was.

It has finally happened. A major campaign for the presidency was based not on party loyalty or on a particular political philosophy but simply on who the candidate was—or on what he seemed to be. It was Anderson's *manner* that won him his support. It was the way he spoke and dressed and looked. It was his utter lack of passion, which suggested a reasoned modulation of whatever problem might come along. It was the emotionless manner in which he walked away from the party that had endorsed him for twenty-five years; surely this was a man who would not be constrained by loyalty to roots. It was his television commercials, in which invariably the background was a bookcase; not a lawyer's bookcase with its even numbered tomes, not a successful businessman's personal library with walnut case and rich leather bindings: it was the bookcase of an academician—

simple green shelves bulging with textbooks and theses and re-ports. It was the careful moderation of his clothes and his prose and program; there were no sweeping gestures, no feints at the masses of voters. His earlier infatuation with fundamentalist so-lutions was even seen as an asset, an augury of how far he was able to travel from the passions of tradition to the calm remove of reason.

John Anderson was the distillate of the new politics. With his candidacy, it was no longer necessary to use issues as a key to the candidate's life-style. Now the candidate's life-style had come to be enough; it was the only issue. And that in itself could be the key to what he might propose in office. His was the politics of pure style. It is significant not only that his candidacy was accorded the fullest attention and respect—the League of Women Voters insisted on a three-man candidate's debate—but that it attracted the support of those who claimed to be particularly "concerned with the issues."

But there was no three-man debate. The Carter-Reagan de-bate may have been decisive in the outcome of the campaign. The reason it was so decisive in so many voters' minds shows us what our politics has become.

The two candidates were rated evenly in the polls at the time of the debate, one week before the election. Each seemed to have almost exactly as much support as the other—among those who had a choice. But millions of voters were still unde-cided. There had never been so many undecided voters so close to an election time. Supposedly dissatisfied with both candidates, those millions were waiting for something to help them make up their minds. The debate seemed critical to the outcome.

When the ninety-minute encounter was concluded, most of the instant commentators called it a draw. Neither man had made a major error. The precision of one was said to be balanced by the poise of the other. At first it was concluded that few votes would be switched.

This conclusion was soon disproved. In the next few days, all the polls showed the same thing: Reagan had won. By a startling margin, close to two-to-one, the public thought that Reagan had done better than Carter.

The degree to which voter perception of the debate influenced the final outcome is debatable. We shall never really know. But the verdict of the public on the debate itself is unarguably clear.

In reviewing tapes of the debate, it is very difficult to see at first the basis of this popular judgment. Indeed, a very good case can be made for the superiority of Carter's performance; he was poised, he was knowledgeable, he touched all the bases. Reagan, on the other hand, looked and sounded less effective than he had in other appearances. Yet the polls were too consistent to be discounted: an overwhelming number of people declared Reagan the winner.

The commentators went back and forth. This time they said it was a matter of style: Reagan had been warm and relaxed, Carter too rigid.

Perhaps. But perhaps there was another factor, too. Perhaps the decisive point was that Carter *had* touched on all bases. He had, with perfect regularity, appealed to many specific groups. To the relief of his managers, he left no one out; he remembered to mention and openly appeal to Southerners, Blacks, Jews, women, and schoolteachers.

That may have been it. Carter was doing what most practitioners of today's politics have learned to do: he was appealing to specific groups, and hoping that these would help constitute a majority. Reagan, however well he did so, was ostensibly speaking to everyone. He seemed to be addressing the public. The public (much of it, anyway) that is tired of being addressed by category, confused and unreached by specialized appeals, responded happily to the breadth of Reagan's reach. In the "us" and "them" of modern politics, perhaps a narrow definition of "us" works best in primaries and before particular audiences. In a debate watched by one hundred million people, though, the most successful "us" is that which suggests all of us.

Reagan appealed to the majority. This is very different than saying that the majority agreed with him. The point is that he was trying to reach people as part of a whole, not as members of units. A nation starved for this collective identity responded to his effort. There are other explanations for Reagan's success in the debate, to be sure, but one ought not fail to note his majoritarian approach—and the majority's response.

Finally, there is the election itself, so very different from all the predictions. If anyone foretold the magnitude of the result, he did not do so in print. Throughout the longest campaign in our history the constant labels of the public mood were lassitude and indecision. Apathy was supposedly so rife that the election would be inconclusive. In the very final days of the campaign the race was thought to be so close that many commentators wondered if the popular vote would go one way and the electoral vote another.

Both votes went the same way. The Reagan landslide was so great—and uniform across the country—that it is tempting to focus on this single race. But other victories were just as astonishing. The United States Senate was captured by the Republicans, an event that almost no one had predicted. In hundreds of other races, the more conservative candidates won. Overnight, the government of the country was altered more drastically than it had been in fifty years. The most fundamental change in direction since the New Deal resulted from an election that was supposedly too close to call.

So great a reversal of political direction has spawned no end of analysis. Many explanations have been proffered. Carter's unpopularity, inflation, unemployment, the hostages—all these things are credited with the result and, indeed, each played a role. But these were not the only things. Other factors helped shape this pivotal election, too.

Much has been written about the role of the "moral majority." The emergence of fundamentalist policital action groups was a marked development in the 1980 campaign. Not only liberals, but thoughtful voters of every political leaning were alarmed by this. Well they should be. But few seemed aware of the source of the phenomenon. The "moral majority" was not merely an extreme reaction to the New Elite; it was following in the New Elite's footsteps. There have always been religious fundamentalists who wanted to impose their will on the political process, but the old majoritarian structure made this very difficult to do. It was the New Elite which undermined that structure, and which popularized the principle that self-proclaimed moral authority justified political control. The New Elite gave us the mood and the structure that permits single-issue politics to flourish, yet most members of the New Elite undoubtedly deplored the growth of the "moral majority," failing to see that they had made it possible.

Many leaders of the "moral majority" were quick to take credit for the election results. It is true that they had been active and outspoken on behalf of Reagan and opposed to most of the Democratic senators who were defeated. They had organized voter turnout efforts and helped raise very large campaign contributions.

But it is a mistake to say that they caused the result. They contributed to it, but it was scarcely "their" victory. The "moral majority" was no more a real majority than is the New Elite. And it endorsed Reagan very early; the polls already reflected that support when they showed the candidates tied. The great shift to Reagan at the last minute did not come from the "moral majority." It came from voters not affiliated with any single-issue group. It came from voters far more representative of a true majority. There is a much broader explanation for the 1980 election than the machinations of any single group.

After several decades of New Elite mischief, the election of Ronald Reagan was inevitable. The election of 1980, like the election of 1976, was part of the revolt of the Left Behinds. To undercut traditional values with too quick and broad an ax is to ensure their swift and wild regrowth. Carter had beaten Ford because his Plains background suggested traditional roots. But that was only one part of Carter. Traditional values were what Reagan was all about. They were the essence of his campaign.

What sounded like platitudes to sophisticated viewers of the debate were welcome guideposts to millions in the audience, so confused by the rejection of tradition that for them its restoration had become the first priority. That and the fact that Reagan seemed to be addressing a total, not a fragmented, electorate accounts for his great victory.

Issues still count, too, of course, and played a major role in the campaign. The economy and the perceived incompetence of the incumbent had much significance. Public disaffection with big government is a fact. Concern over national defense is growing. It is fair to say that the ideological pendulum is moving, this time to the right.

But not that far right. Many of those who voted for Reagan are closer to Carter on the issues. Every poll, taken by either side, evidences that. So it is difficult to attribute the remarkable outcome of the 1980 election to ideology. Issues alone are not the only explanation.

Candidates like Reagan will continue to win so long as the New Elite is the most visible countervailing force. The reaction to one extreme causes the other. Those who deplore the result must alter the alternatives. If the framework and the mood of national deliberation continues to be molded by the New Elite, the results of our elections will continue to be startling.

CHAPTER 5

WHAT THEY WANT

Edmund Gerald Brown, known as Pat, was born in San Francisco in 1901. His father, Ed, ran a poker game on Eddy Street. Young Pat was bright and likable, and even as a schoolboy knew how to please a crowd; he gave inspiring three-minute speeches plugging the sale of Liberty Bonds. Pat attended Lowell public high school, where he met, and later married, Bernice Layne, a daughter of a San Francisco cop. She was described as "the smartest and prettiest girl in school."

Pat learned law working for a blind lawyer and became one of the youngest attorneys in the state. In 1939 he ran against veteran District Attorney Matt Brady and, even though Ed Brown refused to close up his poker game for the duration of the campaign, Pat won. He went on to become state attorney general, and then governor.

From the start, Pat had no trouble in picking his party, his program, and his enemies. He was a Democrat, he was for a bigger slice of the pie for the average person, and his enemies were the vested interests. The vested interests were the rich. An Irish Catholic growing up in San Francisco soon learned who ran things. Everything was controlled by a dozen or so families who owned the banks, the railroads, the land. They belonged to the Pacific Union Club—where a Catholic boy could get in only as a waiter. Pat Brown wanted their money and their power to be shared—by people with backgrounds like his own. If Pat knew his enemies, he also knew his friends: the politicians, mostly Irish, who shared his roots, his drive, and his frustration. He was very much at home buying a round at Monaghan's Number Ten Club in the Eureka Valley neighborhood of the city.

Pat and Bernice had a son, Edmund Gerald Brown, Jr., known as Jerry. Young Jerry was as bright as his father. He was sent to St. Brendan's School, where his classmates were the children of lawyers, doctors, and judges, and then to St. Ignatius, a Jesuit high school. His grades were good, his leadership marked. He went onto study for the Jesuit priesthood at Sacred Heart in Los Gatos, then quit. "I learned what there was to learn for me, so I left." He moved on to Berkeley, and then to Yale Law School.

Like his father, he got into politics early. In 1969 he moved to Los Angeles to run for that city's community college board, and won. Eighteen months later he was the only Democrat to win statewide office: secretary of state. In 1974, he was elected governor of California.

Like his father, Jerry Brown knew where he stood. But the two men stood in different places. Jerry Brown was raised in affluence, his father was not. For Pat and his friends, material gain was healthy, an index of their acceptance by society. For Jerry, material things had no meaning. He found the desire for them deplorable in others, a sign of base values. Jerry's staff and advisors shared this perception. They, too, felt that those who sought material rewards were inferior. "Low salaries draw better people into public service," said Governor Jerry Brown. To want more was middle class, to want less the mark of a loftier state.

He asked everyone to lower their expectations, a relatively easy task for those whose expectations had already been fulfilled.

Pat Brown wanted to cut the pie; Jerry Brown wants to freeze it. Pat Brown spoke for the workers of California; Jerry Brown speaks to them. Pat Brown kept the values and traditions of his upbringing; Jerry Brown practices Zen. Pat Brown was above all else a party politician. Jerry Brown disdains political parties, including his own. He feels he knows what people want; why should they have an organized machanism for communicating with him? His embarrassment at his father's political past is not much different from Pat Brown's chagrin over Ed Brown's poker game. Pat Brown's enemies were those who cornered wealth; Jerry Brown's enemies are those who have cornered votes. He prefers to drop in unannounced among his subjects, rather than to have their demands brought to him as a matter of right by the people's representatives. (So far, the people of California love Brown's attacks on government; they see it as a repudiation of their oppressors, not their representatives.) Pat Brown believed in more for all: Jerry Brown believes in limiting growth (which would, of course, divorce status from wealth). Pat Brown believed in upward mobility, the chance for any person to rise to a higher station. Jerry Brown seems to feel that the present allocation of status is adequate. When a bill was passed requiring state departments to establish an "upward mobility" system so that clerical workers could advance into professional ranks, Jerry Brown vetoed it, saying, "It is based on certain premises that I question."

The son continues to question all the premises of the father. The two are worlds apart. The differences are not those of two generations, but of two distinct classes. The father's class was socioeconomic, with an ethnic base; the son's is the result of his education. The attitudes of his class—its views of the world—are radically different from what his father's world believed.

The new attitudes are spreading very swiftly now, and their impact is very great indeed. It is imperative that we recognize these attitudes and see what caused them, that we might understand the changes they have caused. Those changes have already altered, almost beyond recognition, the nature and direction of our society.

Since the New Elite has no real political philosophy, no ordered program that it seeks to enact, it would appear that all its frantic efforts at dominance are on behalf of a class, not an ideology. Therefore, if it does achieve its goal—the control of our society— would it make a difference?

The answer is unquestionably yes. While members of the New Elite may not subscribe to a formal philosophy, they do share the same point of view, and it is that sameness of vision which would mold our society and to which we would have to conform.

As with every other group in society, what the New Elite believes is closely related to its own potential benefit. Principle is linked to interest. Though its views are often cloaked in altruism, they have in common a selfish base. And, despite a sneering attitude toward materialism, that base is frequently economic.

The New Elite enjoys a distinct economic niche. While its members are usually affluent, they are not rich, but well salaried, without great capital. Their status is derived from the nature of their work, not its rewards. Perhaps most important, their economic expectations are limited—they will never be much richer than they are now. Of course, as they gain seniority in their particular professions, their incomes will increase, but these gradual increments will not convey real wealth. In economic terms, they are lodged in a rather pleasant groove to which they must accommodate themselves, for the prospects of drastic gain or loss are quite remote. They are comfortable, they are safe, and they are stuck.

These economic facts of life have produced a particular point of view, nothing as coherent as a philosophy, to be sure, but a vision uniformly shared. A good example of this informal consensus is their attitude toward growth. Be it in the public or private sector, in jobs or in population, in the economy or of society itself—the New Elite is against growth and believes in setting limits to it. If the New Elite had a banner, it would read "Lower Expectations." Its members speak of limits, controls, cutbacks, denial. They are not reactionary in the sense of turning back the clock, but they are surely not progressive—if that means moving ahead. What they really seem to want is to freeze things exactly as they are.

This attitude reflects their own needs. They are themselves frozen in the economic hierarchy at a place which represents improvement over their past but which offers very little chance of getting much better. In economic terms, they have nearly exhausted their own possibilities, and so they preach a denial of possibility to everyone else. Growth means change and change brings risk. The New Elite abhors risk. It has never experienced benefit from risk. Its own success has stemmed from certainty— the certainty of precisely gradated skills matched with precisely gradated rewards.

Even without risk, change is anathema. Members of the New Elite sense very clearly that no great change is likely to improve their own condition. Things could get worse—they could conceivably lose their jobs—but things cannot get much better. They know instinctively that the salaried positions of millions of professionals cannot double or triple in real dollars.

Young businessmen hope some day to be rich, young actors to be famous, and novice politicians dream of the White House. But members of the New Elite do not hope for such lofty success. Their stars are much lower in the heavens. They know that no glittering transformations of their lives will ever take place. The furthest limit of their professional hopes is orderly promotion— if, that is, things continue exactly as they are.

The New Elite is very conservative on the subject of change. What its members want more than anything else is to be left alone. They want no large forces to intrude in any way on their lives. Their feeling is not at all the same as that of other privileged groups who don't want a diminution of their comforts. Successful businessmen, for example, may resent government regulation or taxation, and fight to limit its impact on their lives. They don't like outside interference, either, and are anxious to keep the things they have. But businessmen are not really opposed to *change*, and certainly not to *growth*. In this regard, the New Elite is unique. It wants not merely protection of its assets, it demands as well that everything stay as it is. Its members see no opportunity in growth, not even growth in the economy, for they regard the beneficiaries of that to be the poor, or perhaps the rich, or both; whatever marginal benefits they might themselves obtain are more than offset by the fear of tampering with the security of the status quo.

For members of the New Elite, then, hatred of growth is an almost holy cause, an article of faith. They preach it on every occasion and revel in statistics that support the theory of diminishing resources. They love to proclaim that less is more, that big is bad, that growth is waste, that nothing is possible. Constraint, acceptance, and diminution are their watchwords. They loathe the idea of moving ahead; they fear the accelerator and favor the brake. Their caution is endemic, and its expression is scorn—derision of any scheme or plan or strategy for building our society or even alleviating its problems. The essence of their creed has already affected public discourse and perception. They have injected into contemporary thought the idea that we have reached an end to possibility.

There is one exception to this hatred of growth. The New Elite does approve of it—fights for it, even—when it sees itself as the immediate beneficiary. Therefore, it very strongly favors the increase of professional jobs. Members of the New Elite advocate with zeal any program or enterprise that will enhance their own employment.

There is selfishness at work here, but it's not so much class selfishness as it is personal. City planners want to see more city planning, and psychologists think more agencies should employ their skills, but each professional is not necessarily an advocate of the others.

In the aggregate, though, they have helped promote an explosion in the demand for professional skills. This is most clearly seen in the public sector, so much so that it has created the misleading impression that the new class wants more big government. This is not the case at all. The New Elite does not want anything to be big, except, perhaps, its own résumés.

This puts it in a quandary. As a class, the New Elite is opposed to real growth in both the public and the private sectors. Its members, however, as individuals, are not incognizant of job opportunity. What they strive for separately undermines a cherished tenet of their class.

These opposing views have thus far coexisted within the members of the New Elite. In the last couple of decades many of them were able to benefit directly from growth to which they were opposed in principle. This was due to the great expansion in skilled professional and technical jobs, spawned by considerable growth in both the economy and the population. Those jobs were *there*, they reasoned, and so they took them.

But this may be changing, given our troubled economy. The birthrate has been in sharp decline for some time, and soon college enrollments will be much reduced. The demand for academic personnel is already quite diminished. If these trends continue, the availability of jobs for skilled professionals will certainly be affected. The very swift growth of the New Elite was made possible by a dynamic economy. That growth is now slowed, and may be stopped—or even reversed.

When that happens the New Elite will be forced to rethink one of its major premises. Growth may no longer be scorned. Possibility may become a cleaner word. But the New Elite has yet to reach this desperate point. It continues to promote its doctrine of limited options and to paint for the rest of society a picture of life as static and hope as nil.

One corollary to this point of view is its fear of risk. The

New Elite strives in every way to obtain a risk-free world. Here again, it wants the real world to reflect its own world, which emphasizes security more than profit. It works ceaselessly to eliminate the element of risk from every aspect of societal life. In politics the risk of losing has been softened, at least in internal party contests, through abolition of the concept of winner-take-all and reliance on schemes of proportionality. In public policy matters, the New Elite's first concern is usually the avoidance of risk rather than the potentiality of gain—an attitude which makes solar energy so much more attractive than recourse to coal or nuclear fuel. In domestic policy, the most attractive word is "guarantee." In foreign affairs the abhorrence of risk is so pronounced that it has led to neo-isolationism.

This is an ominous development. It is not only for the reckless to deplore abandoning the notion of risk. Today our institutions and our attitudes are suffused with caution. The steps we take are small, and leaps are not attempted.

The results of this new national hesitancy are everywhere apparent. Slothful government, stagnant industry, derivative art, and repetitive entertainment are the meager harvest from the seeds the New Elite has sown. What was the most dynamic nation in the world is now consumed with the avoidance of risk.

There is no better illustration of the danger posed by the New Elite. The great threat from this class is not a change in laws or leaders—though this is happening, too—but its significant impact on attitude. The New Elite sits near the fulcrum of public opinion. Its members are communicators; their leverage on popular thought is immense. What they believe becomes common currency. Their perceptions spread as if by osmosis into the fabric of society. Their view of things becomes subtly shared, even by their enemies. Their attitude becomes our attitude, and the alteration of our perception is a thousand times more dangerous than any dictate or decree. Legislation is limited and can always be revoked. Attitude persists, and controls our judgments, our actions, and our lives.

Hatred of growth and risk are general attitudes of the New Elite. But it also has more specific points of view. It is fiercely motivated by the urge to decry all rival elites. Any source of power or allegiance other than itself is the enemy, to be undermined and vanquished through invective and scorn. It does not rank its enemies, all rivals are equally bad. Labor leaders are as despised as millionaires. But if one group is hated more than the other, it is politicians—for politics, with its inherent majoritarian base, continues to pose the greatest threat to the ascendancy of the New Elite.

Here, too, their attitude has been imposed upon society. The vilification of politicians and their trade has been so pronounced and consistent that it has undoubtedly discouraged some potential candidates from running for office. Governance itself has almost ceased to be possible. Expectations have been raised to absurd levels, and performance judged with unrelenting harshness. Politicians have never been popular with the public—and this widespread mistrust was a healthy sign of a free populace. But the new denigration goes far beyond our traditional skepticism. *All* politicians are now seen as bad—and not merely as bad: as criminals, as enemies. Indeed, politicians *are* the great class enemies of the New Elite. In discrediting those enemies, the New Elite has nearly rendered our political system unworkable because its attitude is contagious.

The enemies list of the New Elite is very long. Every rival power group is on it. All other sources of influence or legitimacy are targets. Progress for the New Elite depends on discrediting its rivals. Wealth or votes or tradition are unacceptable bases for the aspirations or identity of any other group.

In the 1950s, when the New Elite first emerged as a distinct class, a book appeared that was very well received in academic circles. *The Power Elite* by C. Wright Mills, a sociologist, enjoyed a prolonged vogue and is still assigned reading in classrooms across the land. The point of the book ostensibly is to expose the power held by various elites in American society—

the economic elite, the political elite, the military elite, and so on. To the extent that Mills's book made the public aware of the concentration of great power in relatively few hands, it is a valuable contribution.

But there is more to the book than that. It is true that Mills attacked the powerful of his day, but that is only half of what he had in mind. His point was not merely that this or that group enjoyed great power but also that that power really ought to be held by the educated elite. He was angered by who did hold power but equally aghast at who did not.

Mills was very clear about what he had in mind. He wrote:

> *Suppose we were to select the one hundred most powerful men, from all fields of power, in America today and line them up. And then, suppose we selected the one hundred most knowledgeable men, from all fields of social knowledge, and lined them up. How many men would be in* both *our line-ups? ...Those who sit in the seats of the high and the mighty are selected and formed by the means of power, the sources of wealth, the mechanics of celebrity, which prevail in their society. [emphasis added.] They are not men selected and formed by a civil service that is linked with the world of knowledge and sensibility.*

This says it all. Note that the rich, the celebrated, the powerful are scorned because they are selected by "their" society—which could well mean society itself. Celebrity, surely, is not achieved in a narrow forum. Power won in a general election is somehow suspect, too, under this formulation, because it happened in "their" society.

In Mills's view, what would be "our" society? His candidates for power are "the most knowledgeable men from all fields of social knowledge." Selected by whom? "Selected and formed by a civil service that is linked with the world of knowledge and sensibility." This smacks strongly of the best and the brightest, selected by standardized tests and academic achievement for the pleasant responsibility of ruling the world.

There was something new and different about Mills's statement, although attacking rule by elites was very much a part of our democratic tradition, and adulation of an intellectual elite was hardly an innovation. What was distinctive about Mills's thesis is that while he attacked the old elites, he was not an antielitist nor was he proceeding from a populist base. His point was not to advocate rule by the people, but to shift the reins of power from an old to a new elite. The book appeared on the national scene at the same time as its primary audience. It's still enjoyed by the same (albeit swollen) audience, though they seem to be oblivious to the fact that this litany of villainous elites contains a significant omission.

The rival elites have been denigrated for so long that they've been thoroughly discredited. To much of the public, all politicians are hacks, all businessmen knaves, all labor leaders crooks. Contempt abounds for every group not sanctioned by test scores. The public has accepted these characteristics because the rival elites have been continuously portrayed as enemies of the people. In books and plays, on television and in movies, the stock figure of the businessman is that of gouger, polluter, cheater—of the public. Politicians are depicted as crafty manipulators, oblivious to any thought of public service, and labor leaders as extortionists and bribe takers. And all these people are supposedly stupid—inarticulate, uncultivated, devoid of a guiding philosophy and led by instinct, not reason.

The argument is never made publicly that the educated elite deserves to rule. What does happen is that every other elite is consistently described as unfit to wield power—ignorant, selfish, and opposed to the public good. The only group that escapes this ceaseless invective is the one that promulgates it. The New Elite portrays itself in a much more kindly light though its gains stem not so much from its own self-praise as from its very successful deprecation of all rivals. The drastic and unprecedented loss of faith in most of our institutions is a direct result of the New Elite's undercutting of respect for almost every other grouping in our society. At the same time, it has attempted to suggest that it is itself the strongest ally that the people have.

Nothing could be further from the truth. No attitude of the New Elite is more pronounced and fervent than its contempt for the Left Behinds. The New Elite sees itself as destined to govern not only because of its own abilities but because those of everyone else are so deficient. There is no limit to the opprobrium it has for those it regards as ordinary people. It advances its own specific aims partly through rhetoric on behalf of "the people," but in fact the New Elite despises the people. Its goal is to deprive them of the power to govern themselves. *"L'état, c'est nous,"* thinks the New Elite. The role of the people should be one of total subordination.

As with every other attitude of the New Elite, contempt for the people has been a widely propagated view. This is the most remarkable example of the New Elite's capacity to create and disseminate public opinion: it has actually succeeded in imposing on the public its low opinion of the public. And the public has bought it! Perhaps not consciously, to be sure, but on another level, just the same; the attitude of disdain, the concept of incapacity, the attribution of base motive, are notions that have infected the public consciousness. An opinion abroad in the land for some years now is that the people are crass and slow and mendacious. Presumably those outside the New Elite who unthinkingly accept this view don't see *themselves* as the buffoons of the caricature, but to some extent they see their fellows that way. The denigration of leaders and institutions was bad enough; the devaluation of ourselves is surely the ultimate damage to personal and national esteem to stem from the ever-spreading concentric circles of New Elite disdain.

Disgust for the people has become part of mass culture. To know what America is thinking, one has only to look at its movies. After Capra's John Doe flees unearned celebrity to resume his itinerant wandering, he stops one day with a fellow vagrant to eat in a diner. Doe is recognized and immediately surrounded by happy, friendly faces. The townspeople express their faith in what he stands for: they recite their own selfless and humane acts that his example inspired. The goodwill and kindness of so many average citizens gives him the resolve to return as their spokesman. The spirit of that ebullient crowd in the diner is worth fighting for.

The small-town diner in *Easy Rider* is a forum of hate and prejudice, with sinister townsfolk jeering (and later attacking) the visitors. In *Five Easy Pieces*, the famous diner scene contrasts the sensitivity of the central character with the hostility of a waitress. He orders something at variance with the menu; when she says she can't serve it, he sweeps the dishes off the table in rage. College audiences cheered his tantrum. Critics extolled the scene as a tribute to individuality; the waitress was regarded as the embodiment of a society trapped in its own rules. To enter a diner in the films of today—to meet ordinary people in "their" own setting—is to be plunged into unpleasantness, ignorance, danger. (It is significant that one of the few recent films—*Breaking Away*—to celebrate the wit and vitality of the American working class, and to contrast that class favorably with the educated elite, was written by an immigrant from Yugoslavia, who grew up watching old Hollywood movies.)

The New Elite is not obliged to rub shoulders very often with the Left Behinds. It encounters them infrequently, and usually in service trades. What it thinks of such encounters is all too evident in films and books and plays and thought: there is nothing to be gained from such exchanges; it is merely a case of meeting one's enemies.

This very frank expression of New Elite contempt would not be possible if it was intended for a truly mass audience. One of the reasons that the general public can be treated so pejoratively now is that it has nearly ceased to exist as an audience. Formerly, there was a mass audience for everything; now there's much less effort on the part of communicators to reach the population as a whole. The audience is very fragmented. Where once there were a few magazines—*Life*, *Look*, and *The Saturday Evening Post*—that reached a vast audience, now there are hundreds of specialized publications each with its own constituency: woodworkers, yachtsmen, psychologists, feminists, born agains, people in every niche on the political spectrum. Each of these groups has a magazine all its own; they never have to read about anything else. Hollywood now produces only a fraction of the hundreds of films that it once churned out annually, and most of its output is targeted for specific markets; the precise nature of the audience is usually determined before the film is even funded. Very few films cut across class or age or economic lines in their appeal. *Star Wars* is a very rare exception. Network television does command a mass audience, but there is every indication that that, too, will change with the ascendancy of cable television. Very soon now each household will be able to choose from dozens, perhaps hundreds, of cable channels. There will be much greater specialization and fragmentation even than befell the magazine industry.

It isn't only communication that has been fragmented; it is all of society. The fragments are able to coexist without touching one another. People live and shop and work and go to school with those just like themselves. Neighborhoods no longer are microcosms of the world but self-contained clusterings, cocoons of shared outlook. In the past, a neighborhood might have seemed homogeneous—entirely Black or Irish or Jewish—but within each one was represented a rich variety. For example, a Jewish neighborhood such as New York's Lower East Side early in this century, contained the full spectrum of employment. There were tailors and janitors and schoolteachers and students and businessmen, and fledgling doctors and lawyers with their share of viewpoints and attitudes. There was by no means a uniform life-style. Everyone was Jewish, most were recent immigrants, and there were not great variances in income, but in every other way the diversity of humanity was apparent. Even where almost no one was able to receive much education, people sensed which of their number were more gifted than the others. Neighborhoods had their sages and leaders—and their fools. The whole human condition was evident; one could feel that through his neighbors he knew, and understood, the world.

No more. Each neighborhood now represents a certain place on the socioeconomic scale. One suburb consists of upper-middle-class professionals. A neighborhood is composed entirely of steelworkers. Laborers are self-segregated, and so are graduate students. Most people used to be in the same boat, but now there are many boats and each has its own harbor. One can see this on the maps of the city planners. Each suburb, ward, and neighborhood has been colored in with a different hue to represent gradations in income or education—or attitude. If the same were done with IQ scores, the result would be a discordant mosaic, each unit quite distinct from the next. Society as a whole used to be vertically stratified: each place had a little of everything. Now there are lots of little places, each with very little variety in its character. Stratification is horizontal now—and geographic, too. We're a nation of fragments, devoid of a sense of the whole. It doesn't matter whether this is the cause or the result of the New Elite. It is the perfect breeding ground for what the new class wants, it is the barrier to the perception that made majority rule possible, and it is the opposite of the condition in which democracy began and flourished.

The fragmented society, in which manufacturers, politicians, and thinkers all target their audiences, spawns the pernicious attitudes of the New Elite. The precepts foisted on us all—hatred of growth, fear of risk, despair of possibility, contempt for our institutions and leaders, opprobrium for the people—could never have gained so much ground in a truly majoritarian society.

The cure for these new attitudes is more than merely recognizing their source. It is essential that we renew our sense of commonality; that we see our kinship with one another; that we perceive that our destiny, if not our skills, is shared; acknowledge the worth of each individual and therefore esteem the worth of the whole. To open our eyes to these enduring truths is to immunize ourselves from the debilitating attitudes that have infected our national life. The rights of each minority must be protected; the framers of our Constitution understood very well that such absolute protection was the corollary to majority rule. With this understanding, governance by and faith in the majority must resume its central place in our actions and our thought.

CHAPTER 6

RULE BY
THE COURTS

Felix Frankfurter was born in Vienna in 1882, and came with his parents to America at the age of twelve. They left behind a wretched life. There was little enough opportunity for anyone in the Austro-Hungarian Empire, but restrictions on advancement for Jews were particularly harsh. Education was difficult to obtain, hard work often unrewarded. The Frankfurter family was weary of poverty and bigotry and of limits on life and hope. Like so many others from so many other places, they endured passage to a new land because even the unknown seemed preferable to what they knew too well.

Life in America was difficult at first. There was a new language to learn. The family had no money. They settled on the Lower East Side of Manhattan, where Felix Frankfurter's father sold linens from a shop in his home and during the summers peddled door-to-door outside the city.

Young Felix was, from the moment of his arrival here (and until the last days of his life), a voracious student. His mind was superb, his appetite for knowledge astonishing. School was not nearly enough to satisfy him so he haunted the New York Public

Library. He read everything. He spent at least four afternoons a week in the main hall of Cooper Union.

These opportunities were free of charge, as was his formal education. For reasons now forgotten, Frankfurter was rejected for a scholarship to Horace Mann, a private school in the Bronx, which would probably have led him to Columbia College. So he attended P.S. 25, and then the City College of New York, where there was no tuition and where he received a good education. Many other sons and daughters of immigrants were his classmates; they were bright and as eager to advance themselves as he. Competition was keen and stimulating, but no one outshone Felix Frankfurter. His gifts were remarkable and very evident.

He had always wanted to be a lawyer. After graduation from City College in 1902, he worked in the Tenement House Department of New York City for a year in order to earn enough money for law school. Almost by chance and without knowing much about it, he enrolled in the Harvard Law School.

It was like entering a new world. His classmates were not the children of immigrants, but part of an American aristocracy. They were urbane, the products of the best prep schools and Ivy League colleges. Frankfurter was at first terrified—a reaction that soon passed. An extraordinary student, he was first in his class for all three years, and edited the *Harvard Law Review*. He met and dazzled everyone, beginning a lifetime habit of close association with the most accomplished members of his, and several other, generations. He was invited by his professors to their homes, pointed out to visitors, solicited even at that early age by the eminent in several fields.

After graduation, he had his pick of jobs. He worked for four years as an assistant United States attorney in New York, serving under the legendary Henry P. Stimson, who became his mentor. When Stimson became secretary of war, Frankfurter followed him to Washington as a legal assistant.

In Washington, as in Cambridge and New York, Frankfurter was magnetic, attracting to him the best minds of his day. His circle was glittering. With some friends, he rented a brick row house on Nineteenth Street and to its doors came supreme court justices, writers, cabinet officials, artists.

A frequent dinner guest was Justice Oliver Wendell Holmes, who had replaced Stimson as Frankfurter's chief mentor. It was common to see them walking together, the tall, white-maned aristocrat and the short young man beside him. They were great friends, and Holmes enthusiastically shared his philosophy with Frankfurter.

Holmes's views on the law and of society itself were quite distinct. Though of peerless intellect, he scorned the role of pure reason. He saw progress as evolving from the whims and hopes and experience of all the people. Progress could not be ratiocinated by even the most brilliant scholars, Holmes thought.

At the very outset of his great work, *The Common Law*, Holmes left no doubt about his contempt for abstract schemes of social policy. He proclaimed his faith in the will of the people as the proper fulcrum for our common destiny:

> *The life of the law has not been logic; it has been experience. The felt necessities of the time, the prevalent moral and political theories, intuitions of public policy, avowed or unconscious, even the prejudices which judges share with their fellowmen, have had a good deal more to do than the syllogism in determining the rules by which men should be governed.*

These are remarkable words, even more so for the time in which they were written. It is not pure intellect on which we should rely for social policy but "the felt necessities of the time." Holmes gave great weight to intuition, even unconscious intuition, of the people as the surest guide to a better future. This view was shared and discussed and absorbed as the Brahmin and the immigrant walked the sleepy streets of the capital.

In 1914, Frankfurter returned to the Harvard Law School to teach. Except for one year as visiting professor at Oxford, he remained at Harvard until he was appointed to the United States Supreme Court in 1939.

His years in Cambridge were anything but cloistered. The most distinguished people in the world were his visitors, his correspondents, his friends. The powerful, the talented, and the acclaimed arrived with letters of introduction. His soirees on Brattle Street were legendary. Frankfurter's real circle, however, was his students. For twenty-five years he met and influenced the most promising young scholars in the land. They scattered throughout the country; as many of them rose to prominence themselves, the concentric circles of their teacher's influence spread. Frankfurter knew everybody. The attraction was his intellect. Through ceaseless conversation and voluminous correspondence he reached out from Cambridge to be a dominant part of the elites of his time—social, political, and intellectual.

There is a reason to recount in such detail the kind of life that this man led for it is relevant to his work. The courts are composed of human beings. Each judge brings a viewpoint to his or her work—a view of what the courts should do. This is of surpassing importance. It determines what the courts actually do—and how extensive their reach should be.

There are two philosophies about how far the courts should go and they are at war with one another. One philosophy will dominate for a time, only to be supplanted by the other. But whichever viewpoint is ascendant, the effect on all of us is enormous.

There are names for these distinct and opposing schools of thought. Those who believe in the will of the people, who feel that judges should be loath to substitute their own views of public policy for those of a popularly elected legislature, are known as the school of *judicial self-restraint*. Restraint is the keynote. It is not that these judges doubt their own wisdom, nor that they lack any notion of what path the rest of us should follow. It is simply that they feel the big decisions should be made, if possible, by those whom they affect. The wisdom of the people is considered paramount. It is not a matter of believing that the people are always right. All judges feel that legislatures sometimes err. But some judges feel that the people have a *right*, through their representatives, to decide things for themselves. These judges draw a distinction between laws that are *reasonable* and laws that are *wise*. If a law is not unreasonable, even if these judges privately dispute its wisdom, the Constitution should not be invoked to strike that law down. These judges try to restrain themselves from doing so.

The other school is that of the *judicial activists*. Activist judges are far more aggressive in deciding which laws should be permitted to stand. In many cases, no matter what the public wants, regardless of legislative expression, it is the courts that decide how things should be. No matter whether a law is reasonable; if a judge finds it unwise, it will be struck down. This is seen as a constitutional requirement. At the core of this outlook is a rejection of the role of the people. The popular will, however clear, is not a major factor in upholding or rejecting laws. To say that a law is "unwise" is to say that a judge knows better than elected legislators what is good for the people.

When Felix Frankfurter was teaching law, the Supreme Court was dominated by the school of activists, most of whom were also quite conservative. This might surprise some people today who are not students of the Court and suppose that judicial activism and liberalism are the same. They are not related. Neither of the contending judicial philosophies is itself inherently either liberal or conservative; they deal with the degree to which the Court permits public laws to stand. Whether judicial intervention, or restraint, has a liberal or a conservative result depends on historical circumstances, on whether the laws being passed are "liberal" or "conservative" in nature. This is a constantly changing situation because the political pendulum is never still. So, at one point in history judicial activists may be seen, superficially, as liberals; at another as conservatives.

During the first third of this century, the country was quite conservative. Most state legislatures reflected this mood, though not all. There were progressive movements in the land; occasionally they won enough popular support to help pass innovative social legislation such as minimum wage laws.

The Supreme Court declared those laws unconstitutional. This outcome reflected the political philosophy of the Court at that time, which generally was intolerant of government interference with the marketplace. But it was not merely a case of conservative judges striking down liberal laws. In order to do that, the Court had to rely partly on its own political philosophy, but also on a philosophy of judicial conduct. It had to announce the right to interfere when it deemed a law unwise. It had to renounce restraint—and that it did.

The Court was not unanimous in this regard. Justice Holmes dissented, and so did Justices Brandeis and Stone. They insisted that the Court should not intrude unless the Constitution specifically allowed it to do so. Their dissents were eloquent, but they did not carry the day. Throughout the 1920s, the Supreme Court, under the leadership of Chief Justice Taft, regularly declared new economic and social legislation to be unconstitutional. In so doing, the Taft court was "activist." Liberals, like Professor Frankfurter at Harvard, decried that activism.

Their cries grew louder after the birth of the New Deal. The political climate had changed completely with the advent of the Great Depression. The trickle of social legislation became a torrent. The first one hundred days of the New Deal produced an unprecedented outpouring of federal legislation—dozens of completely new programs and agencies to combat the economic crisis. Whether these laws were wise or not, they were certainly a fair expression of a public mood that had transformed the Congress from one party and philosophy to another. An election had been held, and the New Deal seemed to be what people wanted.

The Supreme Court threw most of it out—the popular mandate was of no concern to the judicial activists—declaring unconstitutional a very large portion of what the Congress had done. This went on for several years. The Court succeeded so well in nullifying the New Deal that a frustrated Franklin Delano Roosevelt actually proposed packing the Court with additional members—an awful idea that interestingly enough won little public approval.

Despite his problems in getting his plan approved, Roosevelt did finally have his way with the Court. In several important cases, Justice Roberts switched his vote, which caused the scholar E. S. Corwin to observe, "a switch in time saved nine." In any case, time was on Roosevelt's side. As the older justices retired or died, Roosevelt appointed their successors and eventually saw a judicial majority which favored his approach. This was, of course, the philosophy of judicial self-restraint. The Roosevelt Court let stand the legislative experimentation of the day. The New Deal could proceed. Restraint in those days was considered a liberal philosophy.

One of Roosevelt's appointees to the Court was Felix Frankfurter. No one was more consistent in applying the doctrine of self-restraint, and this persisted regardless of the issue involved, regardless of his own feelings about a new law. If the people wanted it, if the constitution did not specifically forbid it, then the Court, he felt, should not prevent it from being carried out.

The important thing, he kept reminding his colleagues, was that legislatures, not the courts, should make our laws. The judge should try not to intrude. Sometimes this restraint was extraordinarily difficult, even for Frankfurter. But he did not abandon his convictions.

There is no better example of how strongly Frankfurter adhered to the school of self-restraint, and no better expression of what that school is all about, than Frankfurter's dissent in the case of *West Virginia State Board of Education* v. *Barnette*.

This case presents the competing issues in their most dramatic form. Like all cases, it is linked to the currents of its time, in this instance World War II. Feelings of patriotism were understandably very high. The state of West Vriginia passed legislation which permitted the state board of education to direct all public school children to salute the American flag as part of the regular program of school activities. This directive was offensive to Mr. Barnette, the father of a public school pupil. The Barnettes were Seventh Day Adventists. Their creed held that only the deity could be honored by any gesture such as a salute. To direct such homage to a symbol of the state, such as the flag, was inconsistent with the tenets of their faith. A lawsuit was brought to exempt from the requirements of the salute all whose religious beliefs were thereby violated.

It was not unreasonable to assume the Court would reject the Barnettes' plea. It was by then clearly a Roosevelt Court; the principle of self-restraint was thought to be held by a majority of the justices. A similar flag-salute law had been upheld by the Court, so many felt this the state law requiring the salute would also be upheld.

It was not; a majority of the Court agreed with the Barnettes. It struck down the law because the religious views of some would be offended by its full enforcement. Even some justices who believe in self-restraint joined in this opinion. For them, the desirability of upholding a reasonable law was outweighed by the claims of religious freedom. They felt so strongly about that freedom that they made an exception to their philosophy.

Justice Frankfurter did not make this exception. His judicial philosophy was put to the hardest possible test, but it survived. The heart of his philosophy was that judges should not substitute their own views for those of elected legislators. He followed that principle. The agony that it cost him to do so is evident in his remarkable dissenting opinion:

One who belongs to the most vilified and persecuted minority in history is not likely to be insensible to the freedoms guaranteed by our Constitution. Were my purely personal attitude relevant I should wholeheartedly associate myself with the general libertarian views in the Court's opinion, representing as they do the thought and action of a lifetime. But as judges we are neither Jew nor Gentile, neither Catholic nor agnostic. We owe equal attachment to the Constitution and we are equally bound by our judicial obligations whether we derive our citizenship from the earliest or the latest immigrants to these shores. As a member of this Court I am not justified in writing my private notions of policy into the Constitution, no matter how deeply I may cherish them or how mischievous I may deem their disregard. The duty of a judge who must decide which of two claims before the Court should prevail, that of a State to enact and enforce laws within its general competence or that of an individual to refuse obedience because of the demands of his conscience, is not that of the ordinary person. It can never be emphasized too much that one's own opinion about the wisdom or evil of a law should be excluded altogether when one is doing one's duty on the bench. The only opinion of our own even looking in that direction that is material is our opinion whether legislators could in reason have enacted such a law. In the light of all the circumstances, including the history of this question in this Court, it would require more daring than I possess to deny that reasonable legislators could have taken the action which is before us for review. Most unwillingly, therefore, I must differ from my brethren with regard to legislation like this . . .

When Mr. Justice Holmes, speaking for this Court, wrote that "it must be remembered that legislatures are ultimate guardians of the liberties and welfare of the people in quite as great a degree as the courts . . ." he went to the very essence of our constitutional system and the democratic conception of our society. He did not mean that for only some phase of civil government this Court was not to supplant legislatures and sit in judgment upon the right or wrong of a challenged measure. He was stating the comprehensive judicial duty and role of this Court in our constitutional scheme whenever legislation is sought to be nullified on any ground, namely, that responsibility for legislation lies with legislatures, answerable as they are directly to the people, and this Court's only and very narrow function is to determine whether within the broad grant of authority vested in legislatures they have exercised a judgment for which reasonable justification can be offered. . . .

The reason why from the beginning even the narrow judicial authority to nullify legislation has been viewed with a jealous eye is that it serves to prevent the full play of the democratic process. The fact that it may be an undemocratic aspect of our scheme of government does not call for its rejection or its disuse. But it is the best of reasons, as this Court has frequently recognized, the greatest caution in its use....

This is no dry, technical matter. It cuts deep into one's conception of the democratic process—it concerns no less the practical differences between the means for making these accommodations that are open to courts and to legislatures. A court can only strike down. It can only say "This or that law is void." It cannot modify or qualify, it cannot make exceptions to a general requirement. And it strikes down not merely for a day....If the function of this Court is to be essentially no different from that of a legislature, if the considerations governing constitutional construction are to be substantially those that underlie legislation, then indeed judges should not have life tenure and they should be made directly responsible to the electorate....

Judges should be very diffident in setting their judgment against that of a state in determining what is not a major concern, what means are appropriate to proper ends, and what is the total social cost in striking the balance of imponderables....

That which to the majority may seem essential for the welfare of the state may offend the consciences of a minority. But, so long as no inraods are made upon the actual exercise of religion by the minority, to deny the political power of the majority to enact laws concerned with civil matters, simply because they may offend the consciences of a minority, are more sacred and more enshrined in the Constitution than the consciences of a majority....

The uncontrollable power wielded by this Court brings it very close to the most sensitive areas of public affairs. As appeal from legislation to adjudication becomes more frequent, and its consequences more far-reaching, judicial self-restraint becomes more and not less important, lest we unwarrantably enter social and political domains wholly outside our concern. I think I appreciate fully the objections to the law before us. But to deny that it presents a question upon which men might reasonably differ appears to me to be intolerance. And since men may so reasonably differ, I deem it beyond my constitutional power to assert my view of the wisdom of this law against the view of the State of West Virginia....

To strike down a law like this is to deny a power to all government. Of course patriotism cannot be enforced by the flag salute. But neither can the liberal spirit be enforced by judicial invalidation of illiberal legislation. Our constant preoccupation with the constitutionality of legislation rather than with its wisdom tends to preoccupation of the American mind with a false value. The tendency of focusing attention on constitutionality is to make constitutionality synonymous with wisdom, to regard a law as all right if it is constitutional. Such an attitude is a great enemy of liberalism. Particularly in legislation affecting freedom of thought and freedom of speech, much of which should offend a free spirited society is constitutional. Reliance for the most precious interests of civilization, therefore, must be found outside of their vindication in courts of law. Only a persistent positive translation of the faith of a free society into the convictions and habits and actions of a community is the ultimate reliance against unabated temptations to fetter the human spirit.

At first glance, nothing is more remarkable about this dissent than the identity of its author. Felix Frankfurter must have seemed to some a most improbable defender of the popular will. The creator of these paeans of praise to the wisdom of the majority was, after all, an urbane scholar well aware of his own intellectual attainments and unabashedly proud of his distinguished circle of friends. He had been called an elitist, and in some regards this was true. He demanded excellence in his work and in his life, and scorned the slightest abridgment of it. His standards were noble and unyielding. He corresponded with the brightest persons of the day and cultivated the most prominent. He did not lack awareness of his own abilities or position. He was proud, perhaps arrogant, and his life was one of studied cultivation.

But though he was surely a member of the ruling elite, though he may have been an elitist, he was decidedly not a member of the New Elite. He was probably its most articulate enemy. That which kept him in the opposing camp was his passionate belief in majority rule. The fact that he was not, could not have been, and was fervently opposed to being part of the New Elite tells us much about the new class. The most distinctive characteristic of its members is not high intelligence or academic achievement or even a certain rarified life-style. If these things were what really matter to the New Elite, Frankfurter would have been its most prominent member. Instead he was its passionate foe—because what matters most in defining the new class is the view one holds of the wisdom of the people. Frankfurter's faith in the people was boundless.

One might well ask why this renowned scholar was so committed to majority rule. Perhaps because he was an immigrant, or perhaps because he had known life in a country where the people's voice had never been heard, or perhaps because he lost a scholarship and attended public schools, perhaps because he had lived among working people and had been educated alongside them. Perhaps because he had heeded the wisdom of Holmes during their long walks together, or perhaps because his lifelong study of history had taught him that rule by any elite, however gifted, was a brake on human progress, or perhaps because he loved this country as only an immigrant can, and understood in his heart and his mind just why it is unique.

It must have been a terrible effort for Frankfurter to hold against the minority rights of a religious group. He was able to do so because he knew—from both history and logic—that in the long run minority rights are protected best not by generous judges but through the rule of law and that the rule of law itself depends on a people habituated to the processes of self-governance.

When Frankfurter dissented in the *Barnette* case, it was regarded as a very unusual event. The Court was still considered to be in favor of the doctrine of judicial self-restraint; it simply had made an exception to that doctrine. Despite that exception, Frankfurter and the Court's majority were still thought to be of the same general philosophy. For a while this was true.

But then the Court began to change, assuming a more activist role. More and more the Court's majority came to strike down laws with which it disagreed. Frankfurter continued to dissent vigorously and with eloquence, but the trend continued nonetheless, and became much more apparent.

The country had changed a great deal. Earlier, the Taft Court's conservative judges had struck down liberal laws. Now a generally liberal Court was determined to strike down conservative legislation.

Sometimes even Frankfurter went along with this approach. He joined with his colleagues—the decision was unanimous—in *Brown* v. *Board of Education of Topeka* which struck down the "separate but equal" state laws requiring or permitting schools to be segregated by race. Even those who believe in judicial self-restraint are willing to reach out and invalidate a law when that law is so invidious as to obviously offend the Constitution. Frankfurter was not inflexible in the application of his philosophy.

But he was consistent. Not all laws were so clearly repugnant. When in doubt, he let them stand. For example, a Texas statute required all labor organizers to register with the Texas secretary of state and receive a permit before they could undertake their organizing activity. A majority of the Court threw out this statute, declaring that it violated the Constitution's guarantees of free speech and assembly. Frankfurter dissented. He was a friend of organized labor, but he felt the Court was going too far. He thought that even the First Amendment should be used very cautiously in striking down laws.

And so it went. The Court increasingly nullified legislation on the grounds that it violated constitutional rights. Frankfurter inveighed against this trend. It came to pass that Justic Frankfurter was no longer seen as the darling but as the obstructor of liberal progress. It became fashionable to say that he had changed. He was frequently referred to as a conservative. Labels became invective, and he was excoriated for the supposed switch in his philosophy.

Of course he had not changed at all. The Court had changed.

The issues had changed. Before, property rights had been challenged by social legislation. Judges who cherished property rights
had been quick to nullify the challenge. Now it was individual
rights which were challenged by legislatures. Judges who cherished those rights became as activist as any economic conservative
from the Taft days in nullifying the challenge to their own beliefs.

Frankfurter was second to none in his reverence for individual rights. But he persisted in subordinating his own views
to his respect for the judgments of majority rule. And for this
reason, he, and not the country, was said to have changed. He
must have agonized at the names he was called. He was probably
embarrassed that on the occasion of his seventy-fifth birthday,
the most fulsome tribute paid to him on the floor of the United
States Senate came from that arch-conservative, Senator Bricker,
of Ohio. Considering the source of each, he may well have been
more dismayed by the flattery than by the insults. But his convictions were unshaken. Despite what his critics charged, he was
still very much a liberal. He knew that the national concern for
personal rights, the new national attitude that condemned his
philosophy as conservative, had come about and flourished partly
because a handful of brave judges once had insisted on the
people's right to decide their own laws. He would not retreat
from that neutral principle because of its impact on the specific
cases of a later day. He knew that issues changed from one
generation to the next, but that if the attitude of judges remained
constant in its faith in the people's wisdom, that faith would be
rewarded through a progressive uplifting of the national life.

The majority of the new Court did not accept this view.
Frankfurter's views had to be voiced in dissenting opinions, and
then not at all. In bad health, he retired from the Court in 1962.
He left a Court as activist as any in our history, and one which
would become even more so.

So entrenched and lauded was the idea of judicial activism
that it was no longer restricted to striking down laws that judges
thought unwise. Courts began to replace the offending statutes
with rules of their own devising. Judges began to substitute their

own plans for those of legislatures. Much of this judicial legislation was admirable, and virtually all of it based on the highest motives. In fact, so much of what was done was so obviously enlightened that few cared to decry the new precedent that judges now, in a very real sense, had usurped the right to make our laws.

The courts went very far, it was conceded, but always for a good cause. In the cause of prison reform, for example, judges did not merely rule that state appropriations to maintain penitentiaries were inadequate; they went on to prescribe just what those appropriations should be and exactly how they should be spent. A federal district judge even ordered that carpeting be installed in a state mental institution. The point is not so much whether this was a "good" decision—the carpet surely improved the quality of the patients' lives—as whether any judge should have been making it. There is only so much revenue available to a state. To spend more public money on one area is to spend less on another. To install carpeting in mental institutions might mean less money for senior-citizen tax relief. Perhaps the installation of carpeting is the wiser decision, but the real question is who should be empowered to make that decision. To Frankfurter, that question had a simple answer: elected legislatures. To the activist judges who followed him, the answer was not so simple: If the legislature didn't do its job "right," then federal judges were entitled to do it themselves.

It is no coincidence that the extraordinary increases in judicial activism coincided with the emergence and growth of the New Elite. It was a trend that suited the new class exactly. Federal judges are not—nor should they be—elected. They are appointed, and hold their offices for life. It is appropriate that interpreters of the Constitution be removed from the pressures of political life.

In this arrangement, however, was seen an opportunity. Lifetime judges, absolutely immune from the electorate, were deemed by the New Elite to be ideal legislators. It wasn't only that they never had to stand for election; equally attractive was their background—they were well-educated professionals in almost every case. How fitting it seemed that such distinguished citizens, dispassionate and free from the worry of popular sanction, should be entrusted not only with interpreting but actually with drafting the new laws of the land.

In point of fact, at no time has a majority of the federal bench been ideologically allied with the New Elite. The former corporate attorneys who continue to comprise much of the bench have in many cases a very different outlook than those who cheer their activism. But that cheering section is there. As usual, less concerned with the ideology of officials than with their academic background, the New Elite relishes and applauds the idea that laws should be made by scholars. Its effect on the climate of national thought is considerable. The growth in judicial activism has had a very effective chorus of support.

The word "activist" has become very significant. Nominees to the federal bench are required to state before their confirmation just how committed they are to the activist approach. Considerable indignation follows a negative response. Many of those who loudly insist on the appointment of activist judges describe themselves as political "activists," too. Perhaps they have not thought carefully enough about this. It is difficult to see how one can endorse both judicial and political activism—unless, of course, political activism has come to mean something different from what its label implies. One who believes in judicial activism can be a political activist only if he no longer views political activity as directed toward the achievement of majority support. If one believes that the point of politics is to see that society does what is "right," regardless of what the public thinks or wants, then the two forms of activism can indeed be reconciled.

The growth of judicial activism was not entirely in response to the heavy demand for it. Other conditions helped accelerate the process and they, too, are traceable to the influence of the New Elite. The erosion of political parties, the retreat from compromise, the growth of single-issue factions, the emphasis on style over substance, all have served to immobilize the Congress.

Decision action from the legislative branch is much less apparent than before. All the change, all the reform, enacted in the name of furthering issues, has resulted in a near-paralysis of our legislative bodies. The political parties of old, large and strong, were a prod and a shield to the legislators they helped elect; they pushed for action, they defended their members against attack. Now impetus and cushion are gone. Incumbents see caution as the highest virtue. The risks of experimentation are very great, but not the rewards. So little is done by the legislative branch that the pent-up demand for change in society finally finds an outlet in the courts. Even judges not fully attracted to the activist philosophy find themselves legislating from the bench with the angry explanation that *someone* has to. The Congress has created a void so great that it's not surprising that the courts have moved to fill it.

This works both ways. The more likely it is that the courts will legislate, the more attractive it is to the New Elite to keep the Congress from doing so. The nonelected alternative seems to them so much more desirable. So long as this vicious circle persists, the legislature does less and less, and the courts do more and more. In the history of this nation, the courts were never even remotely as activist as they are today. The judicial pendulum always swung from activism to restraint and back again. But in our time that pendulum has been pushed so far in one direction that its return is no longer predictable. A large and influential class promoted this movement and hampered its alternatives. It has helped effect a transfer of the lawmaking function of unprecedented sweep, unique in our history and alien to our democratic tradition.

The New Elite may soon have cause to regret what it has done. Perhaps the Reagan appointees to the Court, unknown at this writing but not wholly unpredictable, may demonstrate the inadvisability of preempting so much power to the judicial branch. If conservatives come to dominate the Court, they will find few barriers to their political goals. Those barriers are down, disregarded by those who never dreamed that activism can be the tool

of any political philosophy. The habit of judicial self-restraint—
the essential safeguard against rule by the Court—has been derided
and evaded for so long that its restoration may be difficult despite
the fact that that restoration may suddenly be very attractive.

Rule by the courts may be the most burdensome legacy of
the New Elite. It is surely one of the most striking developments
in our time. Its impact may be even more pronounced in the
future. As those of one political philosophy or another seek to
write their own notions into law, with no restraint from themselves or the public, the immigrant wisdom of Justice Frankfurter
may be recognized at last for what it really is: a timeless warning
that if consent of the governed is not our goal, it will become
our memory.

CHAPTER 7

THE NEW ELITE
AND RACE

The New Elite is the enemy of meaningful racial equality. Not the deliberate enemy, to be sure, for members of the New Elite tend to be free of racism and anxious to expunge it from society. Their perception of the subject of race is genuine and laudable, and flows naturally from their governing philosophy: The New Elite believes that each individual should be judged only on the basis of his or her individual ability. Factors such as income or race are irrelevant in determining a person's worth. And the New Elite believes (correctly) that there are not significant racial differences in general intelligence. In its own view, the New Elite is the most color-blind group on earth. Its members honestly desire a world in which one's race presents no bar to progress.

But the impact of the New Elite is just the opposite of its intent. And this, too, is the inevitable result of its general view of things. A comprehensive viewpoint based on the assumption that all gifted people have achieved a certain visible status in society is, objectively, a form of discrimination against those whose opportunities to achieve are limited by the society.

The New Elite itself developed only when equality of opportunity was assured—for whites, in some societies. It was not enough that some people should possess some abilities to a greater degree than others. Nor was it enough that those abilities could be, and were, measured. It was also essential that those abilities be rewarded by society. Those who did best in certain tests would be the ones to receive a higher education. Those whose educational performance received the highest grades should be rewarded with the best jobs. They should become the managers of society. And this did happen, in the United States, by and large, for whites.

It is from these visible rewards that the New Elitists are able to recognize one another. As we have previously noted, their place in business or the professions or the academy tells the story; the neighborhood one lives in and the type of house carries connotative value; and there are other indices that permit recognition: accent, clothing, vocabulary.

It all rests on the assumption that people rise to the highest level that their ability permits. Even if this assumption were a true description of the way our society works for whites, it is absurd to pretend that equality of opportunity has operated in the same way for blacks.

Blacks simply do not share the same opportunities for advancement. Progress has been made in this area, but that basic truth remains. Blacks are genetically as able as anyone else, but their abilities are not tapped and promoted as routinely. The upward path for the able is a circular route, and many blacks have not been permitted access to it at any point in their lives. The first high grades in school are not really the starting place. Even before they begin school, those children who will do well were trained to compete for sure reward. They were raised by parents whose own careers had been a progression of just such reward; hence the circularity of the process. But the black experience in America has not been like that at all. For three hundred years they have seen their intelligence and drive go largely unrewarded. Indeed, during much of that time display of excellence by blacks was sometimes grounds for punishment. The exhibition of ability is rooted in expectation and experience. The black experience has lowered expectation, and young blacks suffer a competitive disadvantage as a result. This tragic fact can change, and is changing, but in all too many places it simply has not changed yet.

Children from ghetto homes, with little, if any, tradition of or hope for advancement through merit, are at a disadvantage when competing with children of precisely the same intelligence whose parents insist that homework be done promptly and well. Without special attention, it is difficult for an outsider to break into the upward spinning circle.

The same societal forces—poverty, lack of education, negative reinforcement toward the idea of personal progress—that have hindered able blacks in the competition for relative grades have also affected their performance in "objective" IQ tests. This is a matter of much controversy today, but there is considerable evidence to support the view that the standard intelligence tests contain a cultural bias, that they are weighted in favor of those from affluent, educated backgrounds. The bias is not intentional, but that is little comfort to those who suffer from it. No matter how bright a child is, his or her "intelligence" will be assigned a lower number than it deserves if that child does not bring a certain background or vocabulary to the test.

Even more egregious is the effect of naked discrimination. Many blacks achieve good grades in school, do well on intelligence tests, and still are not rewarded with the jobs or the status that they deserve. They are not hired, they are not admitted, they are not promoted or advanced, simply because of the color of their skin. Although American society in the last two decades has improved significantly in this regard, the majority of blacks still face barriers to their careers that have nothing to do with their ability.

This is precisely why the New Elite represents a threat to racial equality. The great thrust of the New Elite is to alter the structure and attitudes of our society in order to undermine the

should not matter. If they were capable of being entrusted with those decisions, they would have obtained certain positions. But they have not obtained them, and so their participation in the political process must be curtailed. As an afterthought, the New Elite will add that since equality of opportunity has not prevailed for racial minorities, an exception for them should be made in the new allocation of power.

But exceptions are difficult to make. When one defines away the rights of the majority, it is toilsome to retrieve those rights for particular members of the majority. It is not so easy to restore individual rights as it is to permit their exercise in the first place. A few positions in the higher strata may be bestowed by a quota system, but to extend the benefits of those positions to others who do not hold them is as unmanageable in practice as it is patronizing in concept. Intentions do not matter because exceptions do not work. A social philosophy is general and pervasive; it's not like a statute than can be amended or repealed. It's hard to structure consequences that are inconsistent with prevailing thought. When you succeed in devaluing the way society sees cab drivers or mailmen—and the way they see themselves—you have forestalled your own efforts to enhance the role and self-esteem of certain cab drivers and mailmen whose color has kept them from grander positions.

Because of disadvantage and bigotry, most blacks are Left Behinds. A system or attitude that diminishes the role of the Left Behinds diminishes the role that blacks should play in American life. Everyone is frozen in place, including those who deserve to be in a higher place. No person should be disenfranchised because of social or economic status; the effective disenfranchisement now being imposed by the New Elite is doubly unfair to racial minorities because they never had the chance to relate status to aptitude.

However benevolent the new ruling class may be toward racial minorities, it will not pursue the same philosophy that they themselves endorse. The two groups do not see things the same way; they are ideological rivals. The basic incompatibility is this:

Because racial minorities share the communal experience of the early Left Behinds, they are committed to the principle of majority rule. This is not surprising, despite the hardship and neglect that these minorities have received from the majority, for we have seen that faith in the majority was rooted in the observation that intelligence is scattered all around. Majority rule is the political response to that observation. It was the bad old days before equality of opportunity that nurtured the concept of majority rule, when people could look around their neighborhood or village and see with certainty that wisdom and judgment were independent of status and caste. The shoemaker might be wiser than the prince. People in humble trades recognized excellence, even genius, in their peers, and sometimes in themselves. The natural conclusion from this recognition was that all the people should decide the basic questions that faced them. There was no way to filter the excellence; to be certain not to exclude it one had to seek the consent of the whole.

The black ghetto is the closest thing we have today to the environment that supported majority rule. Equality of opportunity has not been at work. It is a race that is ghettoized, not one level of intelligence. Something close to random distribution of IQs still exists in these black areas. Many of the able blacks have not been tested and then moved up to a higher plane but have had to remain where they were. So highly gifted people are still working in the ghetto as janitors or dishwashers—or not able to find work at all. Ghetto blacks have no trouble believing that intelligence is randomly scattered all around them, so they need not look to some alien preserve for wisdom—they know it exists among themselves. Instinctively, they are firm majoritarians, for the same excellent reason that most people used to be.

Do not mistake the point. There is nothing good about the fact that blacks and other minorities have been denied equal opportunity. The bad old days were bad indeed in this regard, and so are any vestiges of them. The fact that keeping able people in low-status positions leads to majority rule does not mean that able people should be kept from their full potential. There is nothing dishonorable about being a janitor, but if the janitor wants to become a surgeon it is only lack of ability that should be allowed to frustrate him or her. The universal application of equal opportunity will not destroy the justification for majority rule. Majoritarianism, as we shall see, is not dependent on the soil in which it first flourished.

The New Elite would not agree with that. Its members have benefited from equal opportunity and no longer see the desirability of majority rule. Their experience has been the opposite of the blacks', and so is their deduction from it. The New Elite sees itself allied with racial minorities. How effective can such an alliance be when one party to it is seeking to subvert the fundamental disposition of the other? Can such an arrangement be called an alliance at all? If not, who needs détente? Blacks are quite capable of raising these questions for themselves. When United Nations Ambassador Andrew Young, then the most powerful black in American politics, disparaged the credibility of "Northern liberals" in the effort to advance civil rights, he was not speaking of the liberal ideology. He was speaking of the perceptions that inform the New Elite. Seen thus, his point was well-taken. Once cannot advance the civil rights of some while limiting them for others. Civil rights are human rights and by definition exist only when enjoyed by all. The New Elite is dedicated to restricting the civil rights of the Left Behinds. When one group's rights are denied, another's cannot be assured. Blacks were taught this truth by long and tragic experience, and they can understandably be suspicious of "allies" to whom experience is neither a reminder nor a guide.

It may be argued that majority rule has not yet brought to racial minorities the advantages long enjoyed by others. In this regard majoritarianism seems to be, as Churchill said of democracy, the worst system—except for all the others. A true majority did not impose slavery in America. Decisions then were made only by the landowning elite. Would farm workers, if they had the vote, have established a slave labor force against which they could not economically compete? It was majority rule that abolished slavery. And if the majority's progress since then has been painfully slow in civil rights, would things have gone better by fiat of an elite which limits those rights to itself?

There are those who say that by definition the majority will oppose the goals of a minority, including a racial minority. This view neglects the fact that a truly majoritarian society also extends absolute protection to certain minority rights. In our country that protection is expressed through a written constitution. And the argument somehow assumes that the advancement of a racial minority will be counter to the wishes of the majority. People are deemed incapable of seeing that the strengthening of the parts will strengthen the whole.

What we call the majority is in fact a collection of minorities, banded together in an ever-changing coalescence as regards each separate issue. One of the great strengths of majority rule is precisely the leverage that it does give to minorities—the leverage of contributing enough votes to make up the magic number that prevails. Recent experience provides the clearest illustration. Blacks comprise less than 15 percent of the American population; in national elections, they hardly constitute a majority. Yet the role of blacks in the 1976 presidential election was dispositive of the result. Every analyst concedes this point. Without massive and very public support from black leaders and voters, Jimmy Carter would probably not have gained the Democratic nomination, and he certainly would have lost the general election. In states like Ohio, Pennsylvania, and New York, the strong black support for Carter made all the difference—and in the South, as well. Carter won the election because he carried the South. Yet his home state, Georgia, was the only Southern state in which he received a majority of the white vote; blacks made the difference.

Carter recognized this fact, and so did the blacks. The new president responded appropriately to those who ensured his election. Blacks achieved more real positions of power—by far—in the Carter administration than in any that preceded it. More blacks were appointed to the federal bench by Carter than by all his predecessors together. This larger voice in their own destiny was not bestowed as a gift. It was earned by the blacks through their early and effective support of the candidate who won. It was achieved through their participation in majority rule. The majoritarian process did more to gain real power for blacks than all the past affirmative action programs and quotas and token appointments put together. The crumbs thrown down by the New Elite gave little sustenance to blacks who now are closer to the table, thanks to their own participation in majority rule. (Of course, blacks are far from enthusiastic about how well their needs were served by the Carter administration, but their dissatisfaction was not primarily with access or appointments; it stemmed largely from the state of the economy.)

Blacks are better able to help themselves by contributing to a majority than by depending on the largess of the New Elite. One might ask whether that largess would be directed toward what blacks want and need, or toward what the New Elite thinks blacks want and need. Is the New Elite really as concerned with economic injustice as the blacks who are its victims? Are the perceptions of the most privileged likely to be in full accord with those of the neediest? Majoritarianism does not require that one group assign its problems to another for solution. It assures to each group the possibility of helping shape the programs that concern it. This does not mean that any one group will ever get all that it wants or deserves. We must leave it for blacks themselves to decide whether they gain more through political victory or under a political quota system.

If black leverage on public events in America has been limited, the villain is not majority rule. Quite the opposite. Much of the problem stems from the fact that blacks were not allowed to participate in majority rule. They were disenfranchised by poll taxes and literacy tests (both elitist devices) and by direct intimidation. The removal of most of those restraints, under the authority of a constitution that protects minority rights, has gained blacks access to the process that will most swiftly assure their advancement. We can see that constitutional guarantees of minority rights are not a qualification of majority rule but an essential aspect of it. Only by ensuring the participation of all minorities can we be certain that a true majority will continue to be formed.

Better race relations will not result from the society that the New Elite is swiftly striving to build, a society whose central premise is rejection of the notion that all humans are created equal. A society that denies full humanity to a majority of its members is not likely to enhance the aspirations of those whose humanity is now denied by prejudice or discrimination. A society that denies the humanity of any of its members will respect that humanity for none of them.

CHAPTER 8

THE
LAST ELITE?

What is going to happen? Will the growth of the New Elite continue unabated? Will the dominance of this new class become complete? Is rule by the New Elite inevitable? And is it final? Is this new arrangement of society a permanent ordering? Will people come to accept the ongoing enthronement of their "betters"?

Throughout history elites have emerged, gloried in their dominance for a period, and then been displaced by other groups. Is this transience explainable because they depended on force or superstition to defend their legitimacy? Will the New Elite, because its identity is based on "objective" criteria, on the claim of measurable superiority, be less ephemeral than its predecessors? Will it be, in fact, the last elite the world will know, the ultimate evolution of society's development? An education becomes truly universal, when equality of opportunity is everywhere possible, will this globe be governed not by one state or ideology but by one class, united everywhere by a sense of common identity?

The answer to all these questions is negative. But there can be little solace in this response. The reign of the New Elite will not be permanent, but the dangers of its dominance may well survive even the existence of the class itself.

To begin, the New Elite will change. The scope of its alteration is not predictable, but the fact of it is certain. Economics may well bring about the change. At present, members of the New Elite consider themselves above concern for money, but this is patently not the case. Their attitudes are a direct reflection of their economic circumstance. They are salaried professionals, and everything they think and do is tied to the protection of their comforts. We have seen that, for example, the insistence on avoiding risk is related to the experience and needs of professional employment.

The New Elite has so far been a distinct economic class where income is by and large confined to a certain range. They have identified with fellow members of the new class, rather than with any particular economic institution.

But this could change. A much greater percentage of the New Elite may come to be employed by large corporations. Public employment was the first, though never the exclusive, haven for the emergent multitude of the measurably skilled. But such opportunities in the public sector may shrink—and the needs of corporations are likely to expand. The trend to fewer, and consequently larger, companies is already apparent. Automation, labor costs, and the changing market needs of a postindustrial society have already altered very markedly the employment mix of major corporations to the benefit of skilled professional personnel. The demand for technical and verbal skills will grow much larger.

More and more, members of the New Elite may come to identify with the corporations that employ them. At the outset, chemists or market analysts may have identified with colleagues of similar skills, working in the same departments. But with the passage of time they come to think of themselves as part of the larger corporate family, too. Surely it is impossible for employees to avoid noting that their economic interest is linked to the fortunes of their company. Avarice and loyalty merge. A new sense of identity develops. And no longer are skilled (nonmanagerial) professionals isolated rarities within the corporation; they represent a significant part of the institution. They are not outsiders anymore. There are enough of them so that they can think of themselves as the corporation. The company ceases to be "them," the source of a paycheck; it becomes "us."

The well-being of the corporation will then become a paramount concern. Those things that contribute to its profits—lower taxes, less regulation—become shared goals. The very great increase in professional and technical workers within most corporations might have meant the transformation of the companies by their new personnel, but it seems that the reverse is true—the identity and attributes of the professional employees are changed. Identity of interest alters self-identity, too.

There is nothing wrong with this. But it is a mistake to think of the New Elite as possessed of an unyielding set of beliefs, either liberal or conservative. Attitudes change with circumstance, as does identity. The New Elite has been gaining members, but it has been losing them, too. To the extent that economic interest and shared participation in corporation life permit a new identity, many members of the New Elite will "leave" that class and form more traditional allegiances. And many of those who remain within the new class may come to share attitudes quite different from those they hold today.

If allegiance to economic institutions may shrink or alter the New Elite, so will the passage of time. The formation of the New Elite occurred not because certain people held certain positions based on testable skills but because those jobs represented to them an improvement in status and often income. It was the newness of it all, the change from the past, that gave rise to the new class identity. Old identity had been abandoned, roots severed, and that made new identity possible. A big part of it was the rejection of one's own past. But with time that will change. The children of the New Elite may not be making the same economic and social leap as their parents. Many, perhaps most, will establish households and careers very much like those that they have always known. They'll lead the same kind of lives that their parents did—and, because of that, they'll feel much more secure. The children of the New Elite will not reject their past, they'll repeat it. If they're just like their parents they're also very different from their parents, because they accept the tradition into which they were born. It's a new tradition, but not to them, and their sense of belonging to it sets them apart from the New Elite we see today. Those proud of their upbringing understand others who feel the same way—be they farmers or aristocrats or other offspring of the New Elite. The edge is off, the hostility gone, and the sense of belonging which is the precondition of society is, with the passage of time, more strongly felt. It was never so much a sense of the superiority of one's own peers as it was unease with everyone else that really defined the New Elite. The absence of that unease, its soft erosion with time, will immunize the heirs of the new class from the resentment of society that shaped their parents' lives.

The point is that those absolutely secure about the class to which they belong can afford to loosen their reliance on that class as a source of identity. They can think of themselves as individuals. They can break ranks with their peers. That's why so many Boston Brahmins could advocate progressive causes at variance with their economic class. And that's why the offspring of the New Elite may be able to break free from the lockstep of their parents. A sense of class will be something they take for granted, not the focus of self-definition. It will be the basis of personal, not group, identity. To see oneself as an individual is to escape the precondition of the New Elite.

In many cases, then, membership in the New Elite may be a one- or two-generation phenomenon. If so, then why should something so transitory be considered so dangerous? Because while some are opting out of the class, others will always be entering it. Its members may change but the class itself is likely to persist. And its newest members will always be fervent and resourceful in their efforts to limit the voice of majority rule.

But the greatest danger will not come from the New Elite itself. The greatest danger lies in what the New Elite has unwittingly made possible. It lies in the real tyrannies which needed the destruction of our institutions before they dared to act.

The New Elite, with myopic naiveté, has been opening the gates to its, and our, worst enemies. Through fear and hatred of majority rule, the new class has busily undercut the foundations of our democracy.

That's the danger. It isn't merely the prejudices of the past that have been uprooted—it's all the safeguards against tyranny, too. All the cumbersome mechanisms of majority rule served to limit the power of any one group. When a group emerged so certain of its own superiority that it saw no need for limits, it set about to destroy any check that popular consent might set on its own actions. To achieve this, it altered laws and rules and even the climate of thought. It changed our very concept of self-rule and set the stage for unchallenged rule by a single elite—and never imagined that others might covet this new throne.

But it will be coveted, of that we may be sure. Once rule is taken from the people it is up for grabs. Divorce power from popular consent in order to concentrate it in a few hands and other, rougher, hands will reach for it. If the New Elite should obtain its goal of unqualified rule, it would not be for long. Should the new theory of unelected governance truly take hold, it would not be the educated elite who would keep the reins. Naked force would decide who governs—once it is clear that the people should not govern themselves. So has it always been. If the New Elite achieves total power it will hold it for about three weeks—until some bullies take it away at the point of a gun. The single alternative to rule by force in modern times has been rule by genuinely popular consent. That the New Elite believes itself to be a third alternative, that it believes any third alternative is possible, establishes its own disqualification from the arts of governance.

And if the bullies with their guns take over, members of the New Elite would be the first to go. Their liberties, their incomes, their status would suffer. Despite the highly publicized subsidies to state opera in dictatorships of the Right and Left alike, it is only where the people govern themselves that any educated elite has prospered and been free. For the New Elite to see the people as its enemy rather than its ally is to be ignorant of history and blind to contemporary events.

The dismantlement of our majoritarian institutions will make tyranny inevitable. The present trends in American life are leading in that direction. The systematic removal of decision-making from elected officials, the retreat from broad political institutions, the encouragement of a fragmented society, the disparagement of consensus, and abandonment of hope are just the soil for totalitarian growths.

Rule by the New Elite would be bad enough. But that's not even what we'd get; it would be rule by armed tyrants, once the lines of popular consent have been cut. The real danger posed by the New Elite is that it thinks it benefits from the death of democracy, so it works at knocking down the walls that keep the tyrants out. Every institution and attitude that buttressed the practice of majority rule has been whittled and amended. The infrastructure of self-governance has been severely weakened. What was unthinkable is now possible and soon will be apparent: the capacity to dispense with the consent of the governed.

This baleful augury may seem excessive to some, these possibilities too dire. Even though our most fundamental institutions have been unquestionably altered, it is difficult and surely painful to be certain that the very worst consequences will follow. And perhaps they will not. But we do know, and can roughly measure, the deep anxiety of the people when faced by such pervasive change. The public opinion polls record unprecedented lack of faith in our institutions and in ourselves. The "malaise" of which it was recently fashionable to speak is real enough. The people are, as always, more astute than the experts about their own needs, and the sense of helplessness and alienation is very strong and growing stronger still. Such widely-held despair itself is both a warning and an incubator of the greater dangers that may come. There are grounds enough and time as well, to halt and reverse the drift. The effort can and must be made to restore the safeguards to our system.

To fight back, it is first necessary to see clearly the nature of the problem. All the confusing rhetoric should not obscure this central fact: the basic issue is that of majority rule. Every proposal to "reform" our institution should be judged by its real, not claimed, effect on the people's capacity to govern themselves. When that effect is difficult to determine, caution is appropriate.

But more than reluctance is called for. A positive effort must be made to strengthen our majoritarian institutions. This is an obvious step, and a simple one, too, but it requires a certain amount of courage. The enemies of majority rule have succeeded in cloaking their cause in the language of its victims. They have reversed the labels. Those institutions which most assure self-governance have been the most derided as closed and unresponsive. Repeated calumny has made them suspect. Citizens have been taught to scorn precisely those things which can best serve them. "Politics" is now the most opprobrious word in the language, and this is no accident; it's deliberate. It is necessary for the enemies of democracy to discredit politics through ridicule, because the political process is the surest antidote to their own ascendancy.

What's needed more than anything else right now is the courage to withstand fashion. The single most important step that can be taken to reverse the retreat from majority rule is the strengthening of our political parties. Those weakened relics, maligned and dismantled and abandoned, chimerical shells, the focus of national disdain, need not have run their course. They can still be what they never really were, the structure of national expression—and renewal.

If people are to govern themselves, they need a framework to do so. We can't all stand in a plaza and shout. There has to be some mechanism for consensus and, when consensus isn't possible, for choosing sides. Political parties are despised not because they don't work but because some people suspect that they *can*. They were rife with faults and abuse in the past, but we can return to the essence without repeating the errors. What's called for is a restoration not of bosses but of voters. If one-tenth the time and energy spent on jogging was dedicated to the meeting of neighbors in a structured political setting, our will and our destiny would no longer be in doubt. If one believes that ultimate decisions should be made by the people, then it's criminal to deny to the people the best avenue for their resolve. Politics has been characterized as the enemy of the people, and so it's abhorred by many decent citizens. But that's the perversion of politics; the real thing works—it's the secret prayer of most people on this planet, of those who would die to achieve that which we're discarding. Politics is freedom, not repression. Politics isn't a limited choice every four years; it's the way to make the choices better. It's an ongoing thing, and the more people who take part in it, the better it works. If politics isn't working, it's because almost no one's working at it. If we continue to abandon our most essential freedom, then its very possibility is diminished, and finally is gone.

All the recent reforms have missed this point: For politics to work, there has to be accountability. There's been so much tinkering with the system in a frenzied quest for perfection, so much insistence on form. Most of it is irrelevant. Perfection will never be attained. What does matter is that when things go wrong we know who to blame. What really matters is accountability. Openness is a worthy goal, but it pales in significance when compared to our ultimate protection: the capacity to throw the rascals out—as long as we can identify them. In our decentralized and fragmented and single-issued society, where the legislature evades, the courts legislate, and the executive branch orchestrates a clash of symbols, it's impossible to locate blame. We can't blame our representatives because we don't have any. Representation isn't possible without a political system to maintain it.

There's no such thing as representation without accountability—and no way to make our representatives accountable to *us* except through a broadly-based political system.

People can regain control of their own lives through becoming active in political parties. Fashionable or not, those parties are the only real alternative to single-issue dominance. They're the only way to achieve a majoritarian consensus. This can't happen, though, until the process of participation is made simpler. The convoluted growth of recent years must be pruned. The first political right to be demanded is the right to comprehend the process.

The return to majoritarian politics must not mean a limitation of minority rights. The more we confine our disputes to the ballot box, the more essential it becomes to uphold our Constitutional guarantees. Some rights are—and should be—inviolate from the whims of the electorate, and the return to majoritarianism must be accompanied by reverence for its exceptions.

But return we must. And this is not merely a question of changing habits and rules and actions. *What we think is as important as what we do.* We cannot return to majority rule without the attitude that sustains it. No plan of action makes the slightest sense unless we share some premises. We must rid ourselves of the negative inroads on our thoughts in recent years. We must believe in the wisdom of our peers. We must find a role for compromise. We must refuse to proclaim the limits on possibility. We must lower our expectations for each particular cause and raise them vastly for our general goals. We must see above all that we are one, and that if we cannot move together then we will not move at all.

The future of our country is up for grabs. Politically, the group that will prevail is that which most clearly identifies itself with the need to return to majority rule. The Reagan landslide was said to reflect a growing conservatism of the people, but it was far more than that. It was the desperate search for an alternative by those of many political philosophies who sensed and feared the fragmentation of society. The new administration may or may not assuage those fears. The rival party may or may not be able to regroup itself as a vehicle of majority rule. We do not know who will succeed, but we do know that liberal or conservative philosophies are not the primary issue. The path we take matters far less than the principle that we take it together. Whoever touches best this central glory of our past will provide the saving link to our future.

David Lebedoff, widely regarded as a shrewd observer of the American political scene, was born in Minneapolis, attended public schools there, and was graduated from the University of Minnesota, where he is now a regent, and Harvard Law School. Since then, he has devoted his time equally to political activity, practicing law, and writing.

Lebedoff, who has remarked that he is "probably the last person in America who believes political parties are the hope and not the curse of our system," has been an active participant, often chairman, of dozens of campaigns for local, state, and national candidates, and for a number of years was treasurer of Minnesota's Democratic-Farmer-Labor Party. He has written countless political speeches and brochures, has had articles published in *Esquire*, *Harper's*, and *The Washington Post*, and has two books to his credit: *The 21st Ballot* and *Ward Number Six*.

He and his wife Randy, also a lawyer, make their home in Minneapolis.